THE
ACADEMY

Celebrating the work of John Simpson at the
Walsh Family Hall, University of Notre Dame, Indiana

TRIGLYPH
BOOKS

This book is dedicated to

Matthew and Joyce Walsh

and to all the donors who made this
new architectural contribution to the
University of Notre Dame possible.

The flame of excellence can only
be kept alight with the support
of individuals who cherish it.

A list of major donors who contributed to the Walsh Family Hall
can be found on page 170.

THE
ACADEMY

Celebrating the work of John Simpson at the
Walsh Family Hall, University of Notre Dame, Indiana

Preface by Matthew and Joyce Walsh

Written by Clive Aslet

Contributions by Michael Lykoudis, John Simpson and others

TRIGLYPH
BOOKS

ARCHIT

Pages 4-12: Captions on page 174.

Following page: Study for the Alberti statue, South Bend Indiana, showing original scheme with fountain and basin. Alexander Stoddart, 2017. Pencil 5 1/2" x 8 1/4

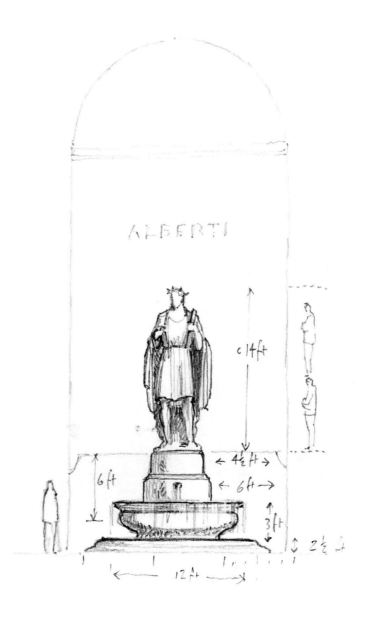

ALBERTI

c 14ft

4½ft

6ft

6ft

3ft

2½ft

12ft

CONTENTS

PREFACE

Joyce and Matthew have a long history of association with the University of Notre Dame du Lac. Matthew is a graduate of the class of 1968 and he and his wife of 50 some years were married the following year in the Log Chapel at the University. Matthew received his law degree from Loyola University in Chicago a few years later and immediately began work at his family's construction company. Over the succeeding years he and his brother built that firm into one of the preeminent construction firms in North America. The family's association with the University continued some years later when their daughter was accepted into the school. During her later college years their daughter met her husband, Michael Gibbons and they were married shortly after graduation. Next year their oldest child, Matt and Joyce's oldest grandchild, will begin her term at Notre Dame. There are other grandchildren with similar aspirations. Son Sean completed his graduate degree at Notre Dame in the Business School.

Over twenty years ago Matt and Joyce joined the Advisory Council for the School of Architecture at Notre Dame. It was the beginning of a long inspirational learning experience. Later Matt became Chairman of the Council and together with Michael Lykoudis, the Francis and Kathleen Rooney Dean, helped shape the trajectory of the school. This process led us to agree that for the program to continue to flourish, and achieve the dreams of the entire Council and the University, a new inspirational building needed to be created. Fortuitously the selection process for lead Architecture firm led us to John Simpson Architects. John and his team with their complete knowledge of classical architecture created a design that will live for the ages and be both a wonderful place to study and a place to be studied.

In this highly complex and divided world, the values of the University and the School are more important than ever in shaping the lives of our students. Ours in an extremely diverse international student population who are hungry to learn both the rigors of classical architecture as well as the life values that the University stands for. All our students spend their full third year studying the roots of classical architecture in Rome. This experience has proven over the years to be a real difference maker in our process of shaping architects and shaping lives.

Joyce and I are confident this new place of learning created by John Simpson and his wonderful team will ensure the next generations of Notre Dame architects go forward as leaders in their communities across the world. For this alone we are forever grateful.

Left: The portrait of Matthew and Joyce Walsh by Leonard Porter in the vaulted entrance to the Hall of Casts, Oil on linen, 42 x 32 inches.

Blessings,
Matthew and Joyce Walsh
Chicago, Illinois 2020

I

THE
WALSH
FAMILY HALL

Clive Aslet

INTRODUCTION

Classical architecture is a universal language which can be spoken just as fluently in the 21st century as in the past. It can respond elegantly to any challenge creating buildings that not only meet functional needs, but enhance the lives of those who use them through their beauty of proportion, the variety of ornament with which they are enriched and the human scale on which they are built. When people experience such buildings their minds are elevated, and they respond to each other because the architecture encourages human interaction. These are the beliefs of the School of Architecture at the University of Notre Dame at South Bend Indiana. Remarkably it is the only school anywhere in the world exclusively to teach the practice of classicism and traditional architecture, as opposed to only the history, to young student architects. For its unique professional teaching of these timeless skills it is known throughout the United States and far beyond.

When the School decided to build new premises for itself it was clearly of vital importance that it do so in a way that lived up to its own high ideals and values conscious that any misfire would be seized upon by Modernist critics only too anxious to prove that classicism is not an appropriate approach for the 21st century.

Those critics have been confounded. The Matthew and Joyce Walsh Family Hall, as the new School is called, is a humane and joyous series of spaces which elevate the spirits of those entering and passing through them. The whole is a judicious set of buildings providing a combination of classical richness and warehouse-like workspace. There is a constant play of light to define mouldings, attractive outdoor spaces where students can relax. There is also a tower. This has created an instant landmark near an important entrance to the campus. Symbolically it is a lighthouse irresistibly suggesting the dissemination of learning and core belief: the light that shines in the darkness and is not overcome. This is the purpose of scholarship and of universities, collectively known as The Academy. The word derives, like the architecture of classicism, from the Ancient world. It meant also, originally, a place: the garden in which Plato taught. The buildings that the architect John Simpson has erected express values that have been passed down from the 5th century BC, in a place that might be described as a garden of learning. These days, university buildings do not always promote the civilized values of the institutions to which they belong. At Notre Dame, Walsh Family Hall is true to the real meaning of The Academy.

Previous page: The Hall of Casts in the evening lit by the lantern hanging between the two Indiana Stone Ionic Columns of the portico.

Left: The lantern of the tower is somewhat reminiscent of the Choragic Monument in Athens, an appropriate precedent as this is the home of the Driehaus Prize.

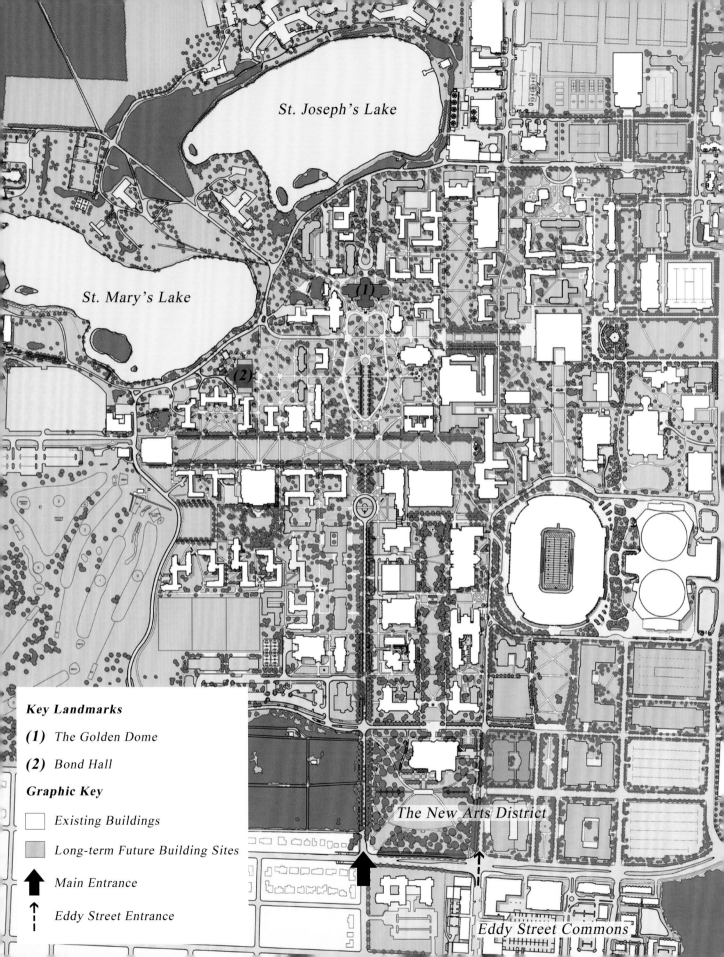

St. Joseph's Lake

St. Mary's Lake

(1)

(2)

Key Landmarks

(1) *The Golden Dome*

(2) *Bond Hall*

Graphic Key

Existing Buildings

Long-term Future Building Sites

Main Entrance

Eddy Street Entrance

The New Arts District

Eddy Street Commons

CONTEXT

The University of Notre Dame at South Bend, Indiana, is famous for its architecture school, one of a handful around the world that teaches traditional architecture and classicism. When the school outgrew its old building, the question of how to replace it, on a new site, was more than usually important.

The school had previously occupied Bond Hall, originally built in 1917 as the Lemmonier Library; the architect Edward Lippincott Tilton had abandoned an early start in banking to work with the Gilded Age practice of McKim, Mead and White, before studying for three years at the Ecole des Beaux-Arts in Paris. His building is a palazzo-like structure, entered through an applied triumphal arch: the steps became famous as the podium on which the Notre Dame Marching Band plays before football games. It is located on the north-west edge of the campus, near St. Mary's Lake. When the faculty realised that they needed more room, they decided not only to commission a new building but to build it on a new site. Funds for the project were generously made available by Matthew and Joyce Walsh.

Originally founded as a private Catholic research institution in 1842 Notre Dame now has a university population of eight and a half thousand on an ever-expanding campus. The focus of the campus is the Golden Dome of the Main Building built in 1879 after a predecessor burnt down. The new building's eclectic architecture, which mixes Gothic windows with Classical columns and dome, would not however set the style for the rest of the campus which is predominantly in Collegiate Gothic akin to that adopted for so many American universities in the early-20th century including Princeton and Yale. Yellow brick is the principal building material. Even the football stadium, originally built in 1930 and much extended and upgraded since, more or less conforms to the house style although it came to be surrounded, in the course of the 20th century, by a sea of unlovely parking lots (sacred space to those who enjoy tail-gating before games).

The popularity of life on campus caused a shortage of housing in the surrounding area. At the beginning of this century this was rectified by the creation of a 'college town' in Eddy Street Commons immediately south of the campus. Originally conceived in a School of Architecture studio the plan was developed by a commercial real estate company and the finished district opened in 2009. It includes resturants, shops, a bank, a bookstore, and other businesses, as well as a variety of accommodation – townhouses, row houses and apartments. As a residential quarter it proved an immediate success. The university now had the challenge of integrating it with the campus.

Left: Long-term campus plan, showing the site boundary in red. The site adjoins a substantial green quad south of Notre Dame Stadium, planned to become the centre of the new "Arts Quarter" within Campus. Bond Hall (2), the former home of the School of Architecture, did not allow the possibility of expansion. The new site is less constrained and will set the tone for how this southeast quadrant of the campus is developed. Long-term future building sites are shown in beige. (Source: University of Notre Dame Campus Plan Executive Summary 2008 Update, courtesy of the Facilities & Campus Planning Committee).

The southern entrance assumed a new importance. Special consideration had to be given to the buildings that served as the gateway from this direction. One of them would be Walsh Family Hall.

The site was created from some of the parking lot around the skirt of the stadium. Whatever went up there would be visible from across the open space known as Irish Green. It would form part of a new arts quarter for the university, featuring the forthcoming Raclin Murphy Museum of Art designed by Robert A. M. Stern (the practice had previously designed the Stayer Center for Executive Education at Notre Dame) and the Charles B. Hayes Family Sculpture Park. It is envisaged that the Department of Art, Art History & Design will eventually join the Department of Architecture in this area.

In 2014, several distinguished practices, including John Simpson Architects, were invited to enter a limited competition. The architects would themselves be judged by the architects of the School of Architecture. No pressure.

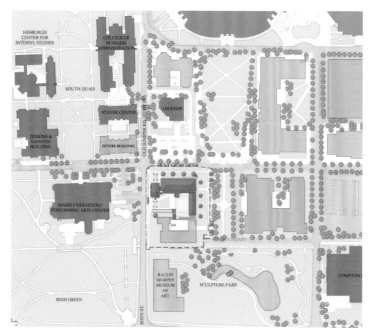

Above: The Campus masterplan showing the new Walsh Family Hall buildings (red) in location. Future buildings are shown in pink.

Right: The screens along one side of the top floor studio provide pin up space and a connection to the faculty offices.

COMPETITION

The competition examined the process by which a building would emerge rather than a finished design. For John Simpson this meant establishing a choice of architecture, interrogating the budget and proposing some ideas of use and composition which would enrich the school as a place to teach classical architecture.

Why Classical? The question was asked several times during the design process. Notre Dame is a 19th-century foundation with a large Roman Catholic basilica at its heart. The buildings are predominantly Collegiate Gothic – the idiom of so many American campuses around the turn of the 20th century including Princeton and Yale (built, in Notre Dame's case, from yellowy "buff" brick that was made on campus by the Brothers of the Holy Cross from the mud pulled from St. Mary's Lake).

Bond Hall, the School's previous home, had been a fine example of the Beaux-Arts style and, furthermore, it would hardly have sent the right signal to the world if such a distinguished centre of classical teaching chose something different for its own building. Gothic might be the default position of the university as a whole but classical architecture need not fight with its surroundings. An analogy was made with the city of Bath. This is one of the most beautiful examples of Georgian urbanism in the world: entirely classical you might think – except that at its centre is the early-16th century Abbey, in the Perpendicular Gothic style.

Like most architectural projects Walsh Family Hall began with a budget. In this case it did not easily stretch to everything that was being asked of it: 100,000 square foot of building which would also serve as a landmark at an important entrance to the campus. So Simpson proposed a two-tier approach to the design. Resources would be concentrated on enriching the public and ceremonial aspects of the School: its face to the world, while the greater part of the building would be simpler. Studio spaces are of the utmost importance since this is where the School's primary function of teaching takes place, but they do not need to be costly.

19th and early 20th-century warehouses could be, and often were, classical. Built of brick they were pared down in terms of decoration, while often including internal cast-iron columns; here was a precedent that could be developed at Notre Dame. It would point a useful lesson to the students: classical need not only be confined to high status buildings. Cities are composed of utilitarian buildings as well as landmarks; both can live together in harmony because both have been created within the same tradition of classicism using the same values and architectural language.

Left: Capriccio of the new McCrum Yard development at Eton College, Windsor by John Simpson (Painting by Carl Laubin).

27

While Bond Hall had been a palazzo Simpson proposed to organise the new school on different lines. The separate functional elements would be treated as separate buildings. There would be a Hall of Casts, a library, studios, and offices for faculty staff. The Hall of Casts would be the symbolic heart of the new School: here would be its soul. Casts of Ancient architectural details and sculpture – sometimes of whole buildings – used to be an essential tool of architectural teaching. This changed with the advent of Modernism in the 1930s and most schools threw out their casts. Notre Dame is one of the few still to have a collection. Drawing on the Beaux-Arts precedent, it deserved celebrating. The room in which they were displayed could serve not only a didactic purpose but would be an attractive space in which to meet or hold parties. Simpson's idea was that it would be constantly seen by the students and visitors as they either passed through or by it. It would be visible from many places and angles especially as you entered the University campus.

This page: Bond Hall, the former home of the University of Notre Dame School of Architecture.

Opposite page, top left: The new Entrance Hall at the Queen's Gallery by John Simpson, is a reference to the origins of Western Art.

Opposite page, top right: The new Portico to The Queen's Gallery at Buckingham Palace celebrates the origins of Architecture. The disposition of the elements is a direct reference to the Erechtheion at Athens.

Opposite page, bottom left: The new, gilded cast iron loggia at Kensington Palace by John Simpson highlights the new entrance to the restored museum and commemorates the Diamond Jubilee of HM The Queen.

Opposite page, bottom right: Hand carved stone and new ironwork detailing on the east balcony of the Carhart Mansion on the Upper East side of Manhattan, New York by John Simpson.

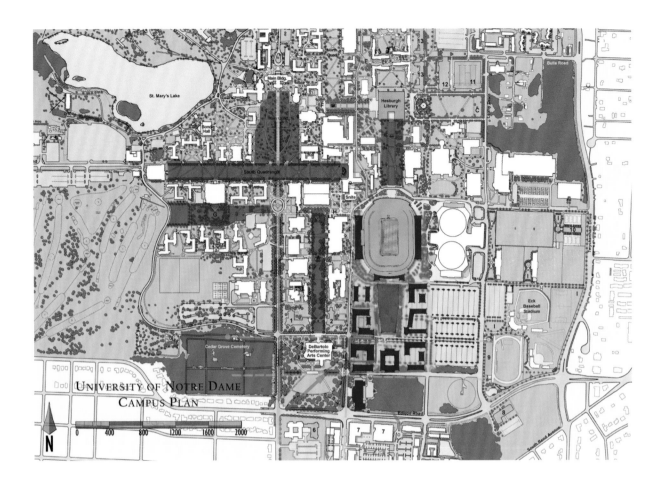

Top left: Analysis of the Campus plan around the site for the new school illustrating major axes and views.

Bottom left: Competition Sketch illustrating the mix of ordinary and monumental buildings proposed for the School. The "Monumental Element" marks the northwest corner of the project site. Contrary to the final project, in this composition, rather than facing north the Ionic portico faces South along N. Eddy Street.

Top: The Morrissey Manor, an example of a small castle or medieval fortress with a tower adds to the eclectic Collegiate Gothic architectural mix found on the Notre Dame's campus.

Centre: A wintry day at the Notre Dame Law School illustrating the conventional Collegiate Gothic architecture with mottled "buff" brickwork prevalent on the University campus.

Bottom: The Golden Dome at the centre of the Collegiate Gothic Campus at the University of Notre Dame.

Below: L-shaped building diagrams, shown at the competition stage, to illustrate how straightforward construction can provide functional and practical buildings that are economic and cost effective. Examples show top left: large open studio spaces; top right: subdivision into faculty offices and seminar rooms; bottom left: arranged to form library spaces; and bottom right: a café and public space configured around a courtyard.

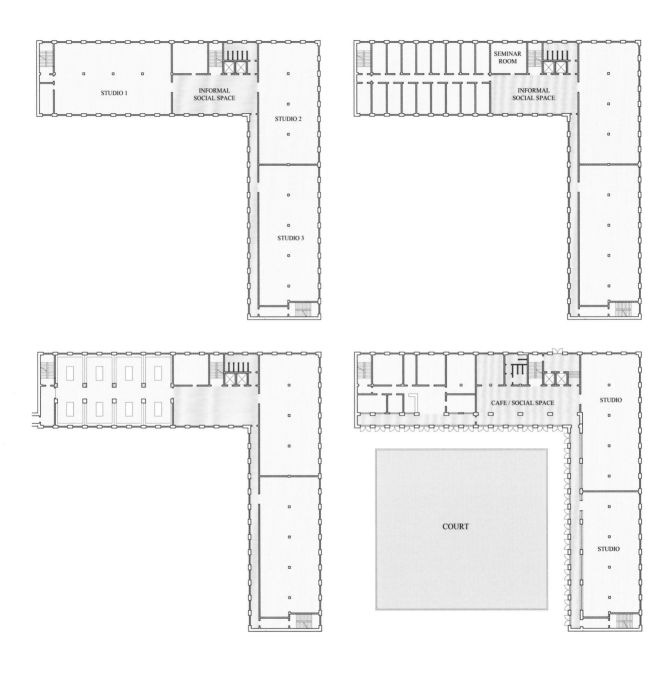

Right: Conceptual diagrams from the competition stage illustrating different patterns of elevations generated from relatively economic repetitive architectural elements. This is not unlike the consistency, order and repetition that generated the facades of 18th-century Georgian terraced houses in London which were often built by speculative builders. Over the years these buildings have proved practical and adaptable and the Georgian terrace has come to be regarded as one of England's greatest contribution to urban form.

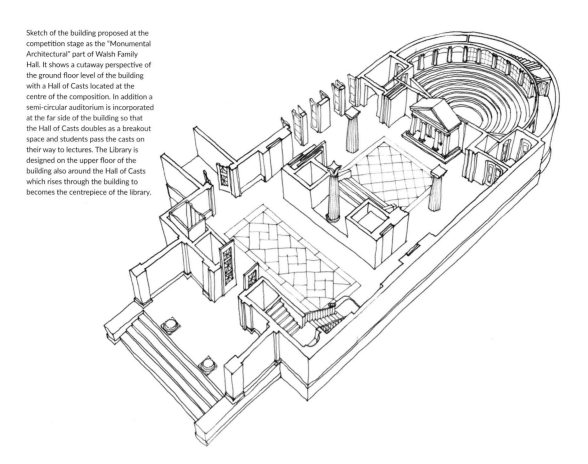

Externally the Hall of Casts would have a portico marking its supreme position in the hierarchy of buildings on the site. The plan was inspired by the Temple of Apollo at Didyma in what is now Turkey. Worshippers who approached the temple could glimpse the priests in an elevated position; they then descended by two staircases, either side, into an enclosed court, and it was only when they turned around – to face the direction in which they originally came – that the statue of Apollo was revealed. In reduced form, this plan was adopted for the Hall of Casts: one of many learned references in Walsh Family Hall which will excite the students' historical imagination.

The studios and faculty offices were planer fare: two brick wings that could stand at right angles to form an L, half-enclosing a court. Whereas Bond Hall presented a single façade to the street, with a courtyard behind it, Simpson proposed a radically different approach: his varied structures would enclose a space that was open to all, which would indeed be integral to the building although outside the built envelope. This is the model on which Oxford and Cambridge colleges as well as some ancient British 'public' schools such as Eton College were developed. As a shorthand Simpson called it monastic. Although this might seem to chime with the heritage of a Roman Catholic university such as Notre Dame there was to be much debate before it was accepted.

Opposite, top: Series of 'cut-away' perspective drawings showing the internal arrangement of spaces within the Hall of Casts building. It was designed to combine all the formal teaching elements of the School of Architecture in the manner of the Palais des études at the École des Beaux-Arts in Paris.

Opposite, centre: Upper level plan showing the library arrangement around the Hall of Casts as presented at the competition stage.

Opposite, bottom: Longitudinal section through the building showing the top lit Hall of Casts space and the relationship to the entrance borrowed from the Temple of Apollo at Didyma.

Below: Front elevation of the Hall of Casts building with its Ionic portico as shown at the competition stage.

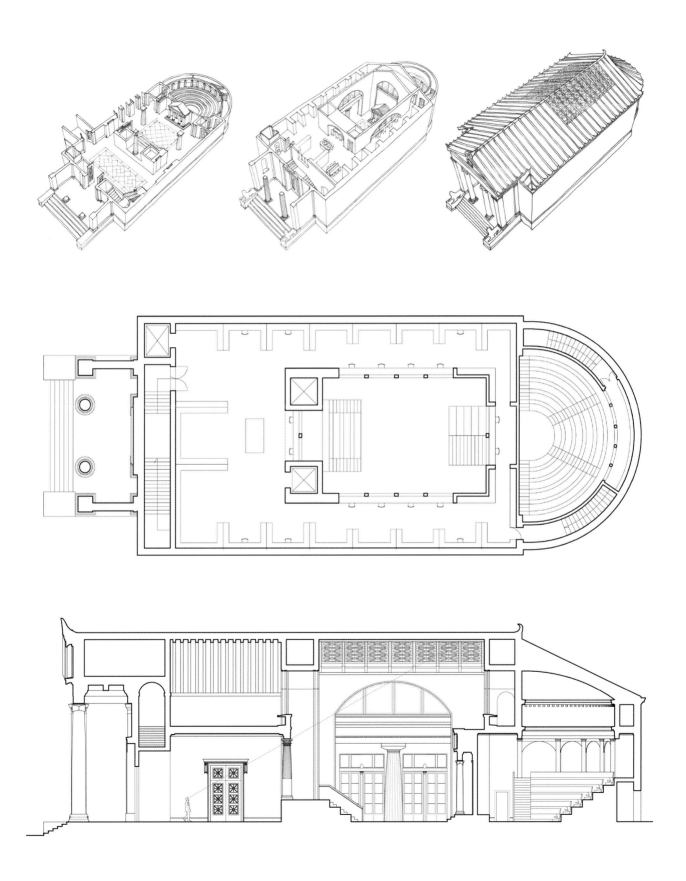

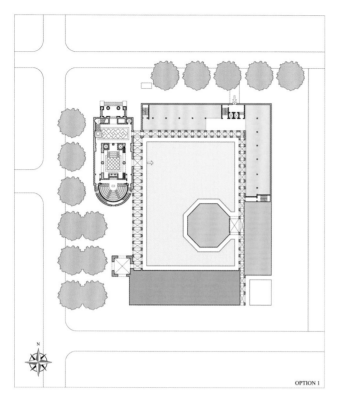

OPTION 1

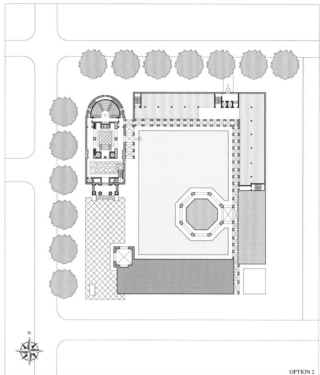

OPTION 2

Below: Sketch vignette used at the competition stage to illustrate the scheme with the Hall of Casts building at the northwest corner of the site. In this composition, the Ionic portico faces the corner of N. Eddy Street and Holy Cross Drive. Despite many variations explored during the subsequent design process, this was the arrangement that was eventually settled upon and along which the final design of Walsh Family Hall was developed.

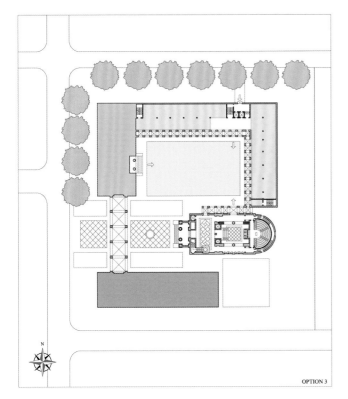

OPTION 3

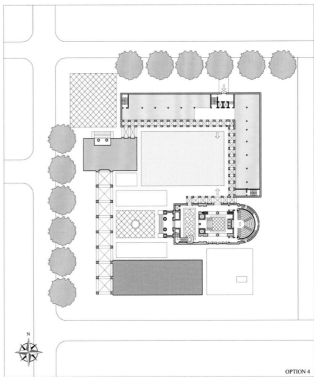

OPTION 4

Top: Series of diagrams illustrating the essence of the competition proposal: the creation of a quadrangle around a central courtyard or 'green'. By suggesting a solution with multiple buildings, the design proposal addressed the existing challenges and opportunities of the project site. It limited the high cost architectural element of the School to only part of the site enabling the budget to work and provided greater flexibility to articulate the form of the School so as to build a better relationship with the surrounding campus.

It also provided the opportunity to explore with the School and the University several different arrangements for the buildings and achieve a solution that suited them best. Multiple buildings also provided an architectural hierarchy of ordinary 'background' buildings (pink) and 'monumental' architecture with provision for additions in the future (red buildings).

Below: Side Elevation to the Hall of Casts Building as submitted at competition stage.

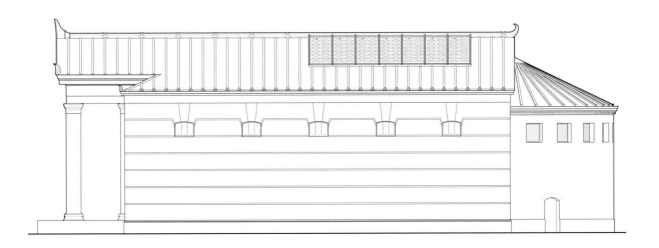

EVOLUTION

After the competition discussion began with the client and the design started to take shape. There were, in effect, two clients: the University Facilities Department who oversee every university project and keep a particular eye on standards and efficiency, and the Faculty that would be occupying the end building. Were this, say, the Department of Chemistry one might not expect the Faculty to have been intensely involved in the design process; not so the School of Architecture. Needless to say there were many views. They explain the many evolutions that the design went through before it was agreed.

The brief, as often happens when a project gets underway, grew in complexity. A new component was added in the form of a new building for the Department of Art, Art History & Design. This was accommodated within the design although the funding has not yet been found to build it. It will, if realised, occupy what is now a lawn along the southern edge of the site creating a further sense of enclosure for the court.

The palazzo idea died hard. Numerous designs were made to investigate the possible benefits it might have over a 'monastic' scheme around a court. Simpson's point was only made after he had produced a tick box chart to demonstrate the merits of different approaches, although some observers may have suspected *parti pris*: instead of ticks, the marking was done with anthemia.

The court itself developed into a space on two levels. This in part reflects a division of the architecture into 'public' and 'private' spaces. The public spaces are on the ground floor: these include reception areas, exhibition spaces and lecture hall which people from outside the School can visit. Studio, teaching and library spaces are above. The division means that a stepped amphitheatre-like terrace (and, for universal access, a ramp) deal visually with the change of levels: but these were viewed as an enhancement of the scheme. One of the almost sacred features of Bond Hall had been its perron, on which bands play before football games and student commencement ceremonies are held. The steps of the new building replicate that function, as well as providing somewhere for students to sit in the open air during the summer months.

How would the site be entered? This was an important question in view of the site's role as a gateway to the campus visible from across Irish Green. One idea was that the Hall of Casts might stand at an angle. The thought of an important building not conforming to the grid on which the university is planned caused considerable discomfort in some minds. To Simpson who, being British, had grown up in the tradition of the Picturesque, the informality seemed natural. It was still rejected: but for

Left: View looking into the court through the glazed transcenae screen. The Tower provides a backdrop to an amphitheatre-like structure in the court that can be used for functions such as commencement ceremonies.

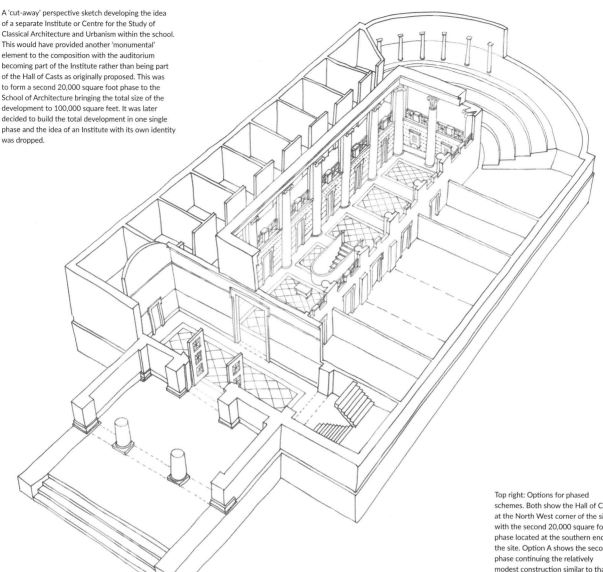

A 'cut-away' perspective sketch developing the idea of a separate Institute or Centre for the Study of Classical Architecture and Urbanism within the school. This would have provided another 'monumental' element to the composition with the auditorium becoming part of the Institute rather than being part of the Hall of Casts as originally proposed. This was to form a second 20,000 square foot phase to the School of Architecture bringing the total size of the development to 100,000 square feet. It was later decided to build the total development in one single phase and the idea of an Institute with its own identity was dropped.

Top right: Options for phased schemes. Both show the Hall of Casts at the North West corner of the site with the second 20,000 square foot phase located at the southern end of the site. Option A shows the second phase continuing the relatively modest construction similar to that proposed for the internal court at the North East. The red brick buildings show the auditorium and the library. (watercolour by Chris Draper).

Bottom right: Option B for the phased scheme shows the Institute building as a second phase to the development. This would have provided another building of monumental character and given the Institute a separate identity. Subsequently, the subdivision into phases was dropped as Matthew and Joyce Walsh generously provided the additional funding to build all 100,000 square feet at once. The Southern end of the site was then reserved for a future fine arts building that would complete the southern side of the court. (watercolour by Chris Draper).

the happy reason that another solution to the need of an architectural statement had been found. This came from the donors, who proposed, and have generously funded, a tower.

Writing about the tower in *The Architecture of John Simpson: the Timeless Language of Classicism*, the late Professor David Watkin was reminded of the Choragic Monument of Lysicrates in Athens: 'an appropriate precedent as Notre Dame is the home of the Driehaus Prize; the award itself, given to an architect whose work embodies the highest ideals of traditional and classical architecture in contemporary society, is given in the form of the monument in miniature.'

Analysis looking at the pros and cons for different arrangements for the school. Each option was ranked and scored according to a number of criteria such as: ratio of external wall to floor area; ratio of high to low specification areas; ease of functional subdivision and flexibility of use; sustainability and reliance on artificial ventilation and lighting; clarity of architectural concept; efficiency and size of footprint in relation to site. On balance this showed that the 'monastic' arrangement with multiple buildings provided the most sustainable and flexible option. The institute is shown in blue as a separate phase.

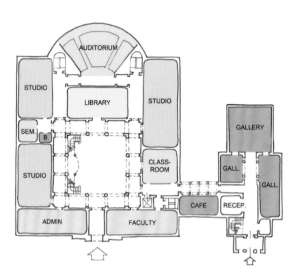

PALAZZO WITH CORTILE

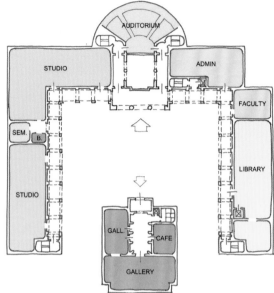

PALACE

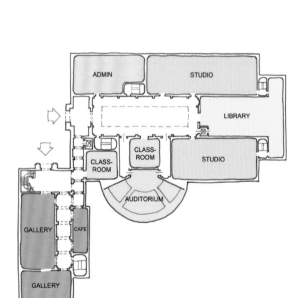

PALAZZO

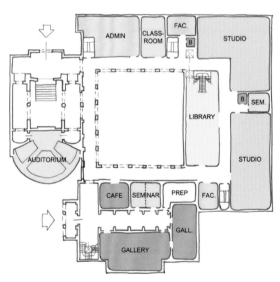

MONASTIC

Top and Centre: Elevations of an option designed to explore the possibility of having an enclosed courtyard. These were presented to the Board of Trustees in April 2015 during the concept design stage. (watercolours by Qing Xue)

Bottom: Plan for an enclosed court arrangement. The Hall of Casts building has been positioned so as to face the main entrance into the University campus looking across Irish Green. The library building is located along the east side of the site with the main studio block running along the north side to take advantage of the north light. A tower positioned at the North Western corner arose as an idea that would mark this area as the new 'Arts quarter' on campus. The Hall of Casts breaks with the orthogonal geometry of the site to enclose the central court and allow it to stand out as the most significant part of the School.

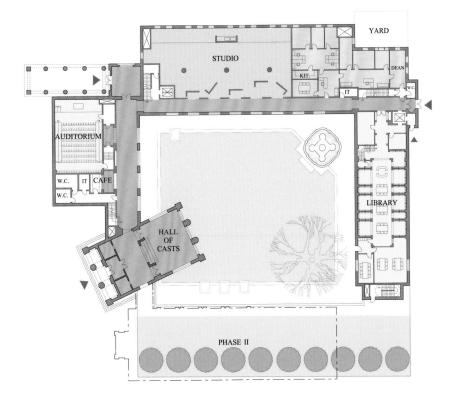

Originally the lecture hall was proposed as an Odeon, on the Greek model, with seating arranged in a semicircle. This was rejected as impractical by some lecturers worried that students would have difficulty in seeing PowerPoint presentations on the screen.

Quite late in the process emerged the idea that the different functions of the School could be linked by a Stoa. In Ancient Greece a stoa is a covered colonnade for public use usually alongside a market or agora (meeting place of the city). It lends its name to the Stoic school of philosophy, whose teachers used to meet in the Painted Stoa in Athens. This would form the spine of the northern wing; the spine of the Stoa itself being a row of Ionic columns (they serve the structural purpose of supporting a wall above). As the architecture of the Stoa evolved, it became integrated so that it worked as the heart of the School around which all the major teaching facilities were arranged with the Hall of Casts at one end and the library at the other.

Top left: Perspective view of the scheme with an enclosed court. It shows the Hall of Casts next to the Institute so that they both share a formal square off Eddy Street facing Irish Green. (watercolour by Chris Draper)

Bottom left: Perspective view of the enclosed court looking at the Hall of Casts. The building has a glazed portico facing the court so that the casts can be seen from the buildings forming the court. It was envisaged at the time that some larger and more durable fragments of building made of stone or faience in the cast collection may be located within the courtyard. (watercolour by Chris Draper)

This page: Final scheme with the Tower at the centre of the court and the Hall of Casts at the North West corner of the site. Perspective showing the view looking towards the northwest corner as seen from within campus. The future Art, Art History & Design building can be seen in the background, just left of the DeBartolo Performing Arts centre in the foreground. (watercolour by Chris Draper)

Naturally, in a project of this kind, funding was key. The last problems of the design were overcome when the Walshes, the lead donors for the building, agreed to make an additional contribution to finish the project according to the original vision. This outstanding act of patronage dispelled the last obstacles. The family's close involvement not only led to the erection of a tower but a heroic statue of a genius of Renaissance architecture Leon Battista Alberti. Initially it had been hoped for a fountain, but this was deemed impractical in a State which is usually below freezing for several months of the year. There were also issues of maintenance. The choice of Alberti, whose statue has been executed by the Scottish classical sculptor Alexander Stoddart, is appropriate to the School, because he was a theorist as well as an architect, and to Notre Dame, because he was also an ordained priest.

Following spread: Aerial view showing the final arrangement with a Stoa along the south side of the red brick Studio block. The Tower articulates the court so as to create three spaces: an area by the Stoa with an amphitheatre-like structure that can be used for formal events; a raised outdoor space private to the School of Architecture by the Library and cafe for students to use and a yard for the furniture and conservation workshops that will be shared eventually with the sculpture studios of the future School of Art. A fountain shown here at the rear of the Hall of Casts was replaced by the statue of Leon Battista Alberti made by the sculptor Alexander Stoddart. (watercolour by Chris Draper)

Top: Interior view of the top floor Studio at the schematic design stage showing the space as relatively functional and robust in character. (watercolour by Michael McCann)

Bottom: Interior view of the Library shown as a double height central space with an upper gallery for bookstacks in the manner of Christopher Wren at Trinity College Cambridge. (watercolour by Michael McCann)

Above: Interior view of the Hall of Casts at the schematic design stage showing it as a tall space lit at roof level by a glazed transcenae screen. (watercolour by Michael McCann)

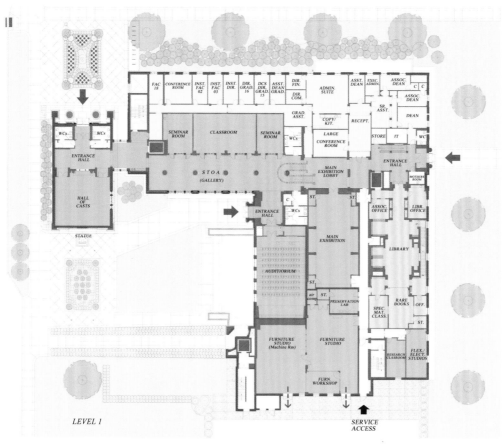

LEVEL 1

SERVICE ACCESS

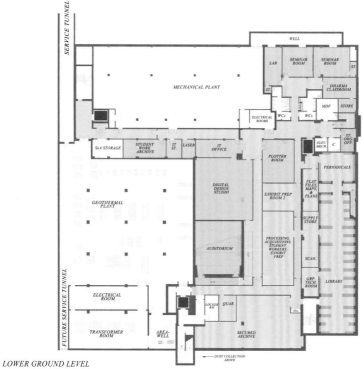

LOWER GROUND LEVEL

The plan at ground floor level illustrates how the Stoa works as the social heart of the School. It is located with the Hall of Casts at its west and the Library on the east and is surrounded by teaching spaces such as classrooms, seminar rooms, exhibition gallery and lecture theatre. It connects the various entrances into the school with the stair to the upper floors and cafe and is overlooked from the studios above. The rest of the ground floor contains the principal Library spaces, the administrative offices and workshops. The lower ground floor level contains a large geothermal plant that serves the building as well as the neighbouring buildings on campus. Access into the auditorium is off the Stoa at ground floor level with the raked seating extending down into the level below. The lower ground level accommodates the digital design studio, archive and ancillary library spaces.

New School of Architecture

Public and Circulation Space

Teaching Spaces

Administration, Faculty Offices
& Support

Library & Archives

Elevator Access

Building Entrances

Secondary Exits

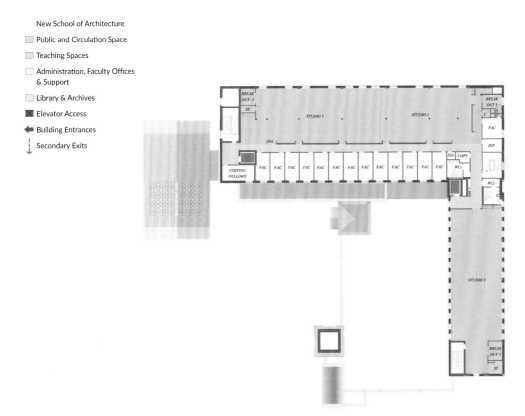

TOP FLOOR LEVEL

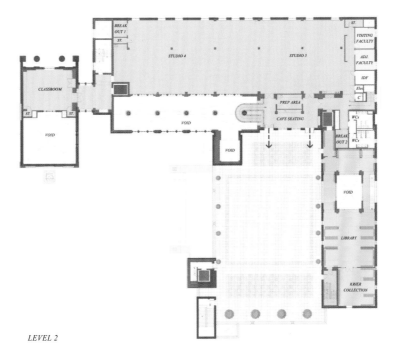

LEVEL 2

The upper levels generally contain the more functional aspects of the school with north-facing studios on two storeys with a further studio space above the library building on the east. The studios have large tall windows designed to be robust and utilitarian in character and provide the necessary flexibility for the students and the school administration. The cafe is located centrally overlooking the Stoa and with access out onto the upper level of the court. The library building is arranged with the entrance at ground level leading into a central double height tribune space which rises up into the reading rooms and book stacks on the level above. The level below ground contains more book stacks, archive space and ancillary facilities for the library.

The north studio range in keeping with the interior draws on industrial precedent using brick cornices and simple, repetitive architectural elements to achieve the economy of construction dictated by the strategy set for the project at the initial competition stage.

The southern elevation shows the monumental rear facade of the Hall of Casts alongside that of the Stoa and the Tower which together define the front court to Walsh Family Hall.

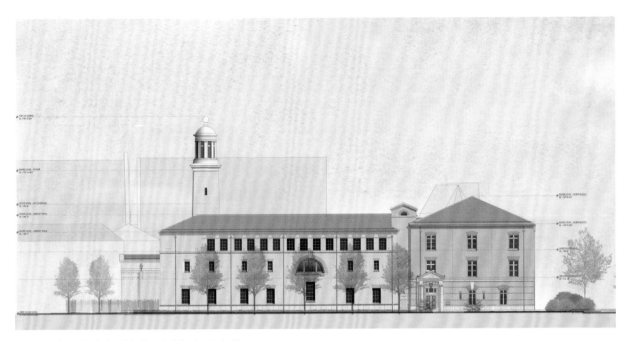

The east facade is primarily that of the Library building characterised by the Diocletian window lighting the Tribune within an otherwise regular rhythm of windows dictated by the bookstacks.

The west elevation looks into the court revealing the stepped amphitheatre that will be used for commencement ceremonies flanked by the Tower on the south side with the lecture theatre as a backdrop.

II

THE
FINISHED
BUILDING

Michael Lykoudis

MATTHEW AND JOYCE WALSH FAMILY HALL

AN APPRECIATION BY THE DEAN

As a dean of the Notre Dame School of Architecture and an architect I have spent many hours over the years imagining a building for teaching architecture. When the space we occupied in our former home, Bond Hall, became insufficient for our needs, I had to consider the benefits and drawbacks of several options and locations: building an annex building, expansion and renovation of current spaces, of being on the south side of campus versus the west, overlooking a lake, or having a view of the iconic Golden Dome. For years the subject would come up in meetings with University officials, and, being architects, the alumni, students and faculty had very particular opinions on the matter.

It was not until Matthew and Joyce Walsh, long-time members of the School's Advisory Council, made a big announcement – that they would be giving an exceptionally generous lead gift to make a new home a reality – that the conversations took on a more concrete turn.

Since its founding in 1898 the architecture program at Notre Dame has emphasized the importance of building not just for today's needs but also for future generations. It was clear that our new home needed to be a testament to that ethos, both a pedagogical tool for our students and an architectural symbol of memory and creativity. The goal was for the Matthew and Joyce Walsh Family Hall to illustrate the importance of unifying old knowledge and new knowledge, and embracing stewardship in the present to ensure that future generations have the same opportunity to flourish. We started with a vision with high aspirations for our new home, and John Simpson Architects, Stantec (the architects of record) and Walsh Construction worked together to make those a reality.

Several sites were offered by the University to the School. The site that was finally selected is a principal gateway to campus and a prestigious location for visitors given its proximity to the front yard of campus. The new architecture building would form an anchor for the emerging Arts District. It is also within walking distance of the new Eddy Street Commons area, a symbol of a successful new mixed-use traditional urban development in South Bend, with much of its urbanism and architectural character inspired by work done in the School's studios.

The selection of John Simpson Architects, one of the world's leading firms practicing New Classicism, raised expectations even further as his firm is known for classical public buildings that fit seamlessly in a given context. Notre Dame's campus is well known for its beauty and we required a design that would fit within the character of the campus while

Previous page: The Ionic order of the portico of the Hall of Casts alludes to the School's previous home Bond Hall with its Ionic columns flanking the main entrance.

Top: The architecture of the portico to the Hall of Casts with its sophisticated stonework detailing contrasts with that of the adjacent Studio Range and serves to emphasise the monumentality and relative significance of the building.

Bottom: View from the east looking at the Library building. The Diocletian window lights the double height tribune inside at the heart of the library. The tall windows on the top floor provide light to studio space.

being distinctive in design as befitting an architecture program. JSA succeeded in designing a building that reflects the unique character of the architecture program while contributing to the harmony of other buildings on campus.

The organizing concept of Walsh Family Hall is a series of buildings that refer to the elements of traditional cities: private and public buildings reflected in their vernacular and monumental character. The Hall of Casts is of a monumental character signifying the pedagogy of the School and is the principle gate into the school. The library stands as a type of middle ground. It is mostly of a vernacular character with monumental quotations at its entrances and windows that relate to the major reading spaces. The studios and offices are represented by a vernacular character as the kind of fabric that ties the two ends of the composition together.

Aside from lessons in architectural decorum, the building illustrates the relationship between principles of construction and architectural form through the walls, openings and roofs in the manner that was outlined by Leon Battista Alberti in his chapter on Lineaments in the *Ten Books on Architecture*.

Above: The Library, view from the upper floor reading rooms looking across the double height Tribune with its arched openings to the main Library space below.

Right: Alexander Stoddart's statue of Leon Battista Alberti (1404 – 1472), Stoddart states, "Alberti was primarily a theorist – a man dedicated to ideas about beauty, formal 'justice', harmony and proportion by means of the word. Yet he was fortunate to have had, by his own hand and the hands of others, the chance to manifest such concepts in perceptual form." (Alexander Stoddart, May 2017). Alberti was a practicing architect, an academic as well as an ordained priest and as such the ideal subject to be honoured by the University and the School.

There are several different kinds of wall treatments and brickwork. The cast stone base and details are contrasted with common bond and Flemish bond brickwork. All the different ways openings of different sizes and scales can be spanned. It is a catalogue of flat, segmented and full arches. Lintels are expressed as both beams and flat arches. The roofs are carefully designed to shed water and snow and the eaves and cornices are emblematic of the building technology classes taught in the School's studios and classrooms.

The portico of the main entrance and the Hall of Casts is of solid Indiana limestone in the Ionic manner. The columns recall the School's history on campus being housed in the former Lemmonier Library for 50 years. The carved capitals and solid drums a nod to both tradition and modernity. Tradition is seen in the language and the modern in how they were crafted using technology as well as craft. The pediment on the north and the statue of Leon Battista Alberti by the sculptor Alexander Stoddart on the south symbolize the importance of pedagogy through observation and study. The portico illustrates the example and the statue directs the student to the first humanist architect who engaged cities and buildings in his *Ten Books on Architecture*.

The construction of Walsh Family Hall emphasizes economy while maximizing the architectural character in keeping with the values of sustainability and conservation for the long-term life of the building. Authentic sustainability is a cornerstone of the School's curriculum – buildings must be made to last hundreds of years, not merely decades. New products and technology are only a small part of true sustainability which begins with the design process and draws from lessons of the past related to durable construction as well as natural ventilation and lighting. Walsh Family Hall reflects these values with sustainable elements throughout the building.

To conserve energy the floor plates are narrow enough that natural light reaches all the appropriate habitable spaces especially the studios, offices and public rooms. The fenestration is made of operable windows where appropriate such that air can circulate freely during those days that air conditioning and heating are not required.

The interiors are spartan but durable with plain, concrete floors, concrete block interior walls and partitions, and exposed ceilings in studios, laboratories, classrooms and the areas of public circulation. More ceremonially appropriate architectural articulation is used for the main lobbies, Hall of Casts, auditorium and library. The terrace and court convey the sense of community that an architecture school aspires to foster.

Energy efficiency was important, and the building design incorporates a new geothermal system that provides heating and cooling that serve Walsh Family Hall, as well as a number of the surrounding buildings, which help to reduce the University's dependence on fossil fuels.

Left: The courtyard has an entrance next to the Stoa marked by a small Ionic portico and doorcase. This leads to the Stoa and provides public access to school facilities such as the Lecture Theatre and the Exhibition Gallery.

Following spread: The Tower at the southern end of the court is positioned to catch views from the University's main entrance and from within campus. It also facilitates access to the top of the stepped amphitheatre which acts as a backdrop to the lower court.

The School's monumental stair wraps around the last Ionic column at the eastern end of the Stoa, returning as it ascends to the cafe and open studios above. The stair is supported by three bracketed consoles that are neither Doric nor Ionic based on the order from the Throne of Apollo at Amyklai at Sparta by Bathykles of Magnesia.

With many recycled materials included in the structure Walsh Family Hall is anticipated to achieve LEED Gold certification.

The building's character looks to the history of the campus. The yellow brick references the early buildings that were built of bricks made from the clay found at the bottom of St. Mary and St. Joseph Lakes. The red brick references the materials on South Dining Hall, designed by one of America's greatest 20th-century architects, Ralph Adams Cram.

The raised part of the court refers to the Italian piazzas that have been part of the School's Rome program for the last fifty years. The tower refers to the many towers of the Italian hill towns on one level, it also symbolizes the Catholic intellectual tradition in the unity of knowledge, as well as symbolizing knowledge as a beacon of light that illuminates the future.

Another aspect of the building that was important to the School was that it should represent both tradition and modernity. While the character appears to be mostly traditional with both vernacular and classical elements, there are a few important references to modernity. Aside from the steel structure in the Studio building and the exposed steel trusses on the third floor, the free plan of the Stoa is a hidden move that takes a while to observe. The Stoa is actually centered under the exterior wall of the south side of the building linking the outside to the interior of the building.

Right: Looking up into the two storey Tribune that rises through the new Library building. With its Diocletian windows it echoes C. R. Cockerell's two-storeyed University Library at Cambridge of 1837-40, owned by Gonville and Caius College, where John Simpson carried out works in the 1990s.

The portrait of the benefactors, Matthew and Joyce Walsh, is not just the usual portrait of the principal donors of buildings. The painting by Leonard Porter of New York places the Walshes in front of the University's first Log Chapel. Several figures around the chapel are fashioning a column out of the trunks of trees in a symbolic act of how architecture comes from nature; this background scene connects the origins of architecture in its rustic state to classicism through the vernacular. The painting is an allegory of the builder in nature with a bird's nest and beehive representing the making of shelter in nature. The Walshes, as the subjects of the painting, are shown as the patrons of Notre Dame and the School devoted to building the future.

Finally the building's siting sets the stage for the development of new quadrangles just south of the stadium. Walsh Family Hall is part of a larger future plan to create an arts quarter as well as a new seamless connection to the city of South Bend through its proximity to Eddy Street Commons.

Our new home is a symbol of the timelessness, inventiveness and appropriateness of traditional architecture and urbanism in contemporary times, a testament of commitment to our ways of teaching.

Left: The Hall of Casts is a lofty top lit space where casts and fragments of buildings are hung so that students can study the mouldings and how they work in defining the scale, character and sculptural form of a building.

Right: A student in the Hall of Casts learning how shadows are shed by different mouldings and how they are used to direct and control the way rain water flows across a façade so as to help a building develop a patina and grow old gracefully.

Bottom: Furniture design with Professor Robert Brandt exposes students to an ethic in craft so that they gain valuable knowledge in the properties of materials, process and three-dimensional design. In the Ryan Companies Furniture Studio, equipped with both power and hand tools, students construct furniture of original design.

Top: Students and faculty in the Classroom overlooking the Hall of Casts discussing Architecture.

Right: View looking into the Hall of Casts through the transcenae screen on the window from the Classroom.

III

THE
STUDENT
EXPERIENCE

Ian Griffey, Angelica Ketcham,
Hallie Swenson

Ian Griffey

Dates of Study: 2017-2020, Notre Dame Class of 2020
Graduated with an M.Arch (Masters of Architecture)

When I first applied to Notre Dame among the many exciting things I learned about the program was that they were building a new home for the School of Architecture. At the time I don't think I fully understood the magnitude and difficulty of this task. The mission of the Notre Dame School of Architecture is unique in the world basing its studies in that of classical architecture; in the words of Vitruvius, firmness, commodity, and delight. When I first applied the school was housed in Bond Hall, a 1917 classical building that had served as the university library until a 1964 renovation made it the home of the School of Architecture. Constructing a new building was a significant move in that rather than abiding in a historic building constructed when the Beaux-Arts style was prominent it was a deliberate statement to the world and definition of the principles that grounded the school. No doubt that a classical building in the architectural world of 2018 would attract attention. Add to that the difficulty of designing a space for architects that teach future architects, and the task seems almost insurmountable.

I started to understand the significance of the building as I observed its construction together with a daily audience of the population from the School of Architecture, the construction site being a short walk away from our previous home. Even during construction it was clear that the building was designed with great sensitivity to each of the challenges with which it was presented. What impacted me even before entering the building during that time was the humanity of the building; the clear emphasis on Vitruvian principles. Even from the exterior it was clear that this building was created with people as the driving factor. Massing broken down to a human scale that also allowed natural light into the interior spaces and comprehensible building forms evidenced the importance of the user in the design. The entire composition being centered on the public courtyard and anchored with a monumental tower communicated the intentions of the school; the importance placed not on the building itself, but on a public space that bids the invitation for all to come and see. Once the School of Architecture made the much-anticipated move, the humanist design intentions revealed themselves each day as I experienced learning within the walls.

As I look back on my experience in Walsh Family Hall I appreciate how the spaces within the building were also created with the human in mind. From their scale to the mindfulness of beauty incorporated into each room, the human emphasis made these spaces the setting for different interactions. This began with the Stoa which quickly revealed itself as the heart of the school. With its soaring Ionic columns, wall of windows looking out onto the courtyard, and intricate detail, the space communicates to all who enter that the school of architecture is a place

Previous page: In June 2014, Prof. Aimee Buccellato analysed comments and suggestions collected from faculty, students, and staff regarding features they thought were important to the new School. A significant issue highlighted was a desire to maximise interaction between students from different years within the school and between students and faculty. Over 80% commented that greater opportunities for exhibition and pin-up space would encourage such interaction but an even greater percentage prioritised the role that the right type of shared social space could play in achieving this. The Stoa is designed to maximise this interaction and to encourage a feeling of community within the School. It does this as an imposing formal space but even more significantly as the informal circulation spine and gallery space so that it is where day to day life occurs at the heart of Walsh Family Hall. (Photo: Scenographia: Live-Drawing Event, Walsh Family Hall, 23-24 January, 2020).

Right: The Café is located so that it is at the top of the stair leading up from the Stoa. View of stair and Stoa from Café.

Following spread: Prof. Richard Piccolo with students at St Peter's in Rome, October, 2018.

set apart. I recalled a similar feeling entering the Stoa as I did when I entered St. Peter's Basilica in Rome – that I was part of something bigger. Reflecting on my daily passage through the Stoa it is impactful to me to realize how it was the setting for so many different interactions: from organized events, like receptions and book auctions, to unexpected encounters with colleagues, friends and professors. The significance of the space was enhanced by all the connections it fostered not just because it was a hub of the school but because of the layers of communication made possible by the architecture. The interior fenestration between the Stoa and the classroom spaces on the north side acted as a connection point, allowing for not just natural light to enter the classroom spaces but for unspoken connection between those that were using it. I would sometimes notice students of other colleges incorporating a walk through the Stoa into their daily commute to class. During school hours I would often walk through the stoa and see students in classes or reviews and recall times where I was in the same position or look forward to when I would be in their shoes.

These unspoken connections created an energy unlike any other, that of the fervent work of a group of people in pursuit of something greater than themselves.

The processional of spaces from the Stoa to the studio also was also of significance to me as a student. From the venerating and monumental space of the Stoa, one progressed through a sequence of spaces of varying scales and finishes that ended in the studio, a more intimately scaled location with simpler detailing. However spending time in the studio revealed that beauty was not lost in the simplicity of the space, but simply expressed differently. For the majority of my time at Walsh Family Hall I was in the studio space above the library. Looking back I realize how beauty was infused there differently than it was in the Stoa. The long banks of windows flanking each side allow for natural light to pour into the space. Additionally the amount of fenestration allows for a connection with the outside so commonly lost in workspaces I have experienced. Here the interaction was with not only with the other students at various points in their architectural schooling but also the university setting. Looking out from my drafting desk onto the terrace, the tower and other university buildings beyond and seeing students walking between classes served as a constant reminder of the school's place in the university. Again it was a reminder that I was part of something bigger; that my mission and admonition as a graduate of the School of Architecture would be that of architectural stewardship and sensitivity towards those who would use the spaces I designed. The view outside of my window reminded me that my knowledge, working in tandem with that of others in the university, would collectively improve the world we lived in. Sunsets from the space were spectacular with the tower silhouetted against a dramatic pink and orange sky. It became an almost daily ritual that someone would suddenly discover the beauty of the sunset, quickly extinguish the lights and invite all gather and watch it. I personally witnessed several beautiful sunrises after long nights of work in that studio as well, but happily those were less frequent. Like the Stoa the energy of the space was palpable; an unspoken connection created by so many students dedicatedly working on different projects but with one common goal.

As I reflect on my time at Walsh Family Hall I am filled with gratitude. I am grateful and proud that the home of the School of Architecture is rooted in design that transcends its construction date; one of an architectural tradition of enduring beauty. To experience a beautiful place like this renews my appreciation for the gift of life and reminds me that architecture is a profession of service rather than fame. Reflecting on my experience I can see that this building exemplifies firmness, commodity and delight, and leads others to infuse the same principles into their work. This structure is one set apart: elevated in its sense of place and inherent in its communication of an architectural resolve. These feelings embody what I aim for in architecture: to be a positive force to all who find my future designs the setting for their daily lives.

Top: Students at their desks within the studio space. The large windows provide ample north light for the students to work on their drawings and watercolours.

Bottom: The Auditorium being used for a lecture during the day with the window blinds raised to provide daylight and a visual connection with the outside world. AV technology with blackout blinds are built in for use when required.

Angelica Ketcham

Dates of study: 2018- , Future Notre Dame Class of 2023
Studying for a B.Arch (Bachelor of Architecture)

One of the first things that the Notre Dame School of Architecture's class of 2023 was told to memorize was the Vitruvian Triad. Accompanied by the seven temple types, anticipating the six chief characteristics of Baroque Expressionism, and far preceding Le Corbusier's five points of architecture, we learned *firmitas*, *utilitas*, and *venusitas*— soundness, utility, and attractiveness. All three legs of the metaphorical table we pictured were necessary to keep it upright; the absence of one would topple the entire structure. As our learning progressed applications of this balance evolved into the famous, falsely dichotomous, Form versus Function and the eventual understanding that the two are inextricably linked. A successful structure's use necessarily informs its form; a structure's form must be appropriate to its use.

To design a building whose purpose is to accommodate future designers of buildings is then to encounter multiple layers of form-function synthesis. So few architecture schools take the opportunity to inspire their students at the most basic level by creating a physical environment that can stand alongside those studied in history classes: an equally viable progenitor of student work. This is exactly where Walsh Family Hall of Architecture does its duty to us: in being itself a teaching tool.

Perhaps we sit in the auditorium where Walsh Family Hall can fulfill its more immediate functional role as an academic building. While in that auditorium we study and replicate precise drawings of Ionic volutes: learning two methods for constructing the spirals with a compass. Perhaps some of us wonder briefly whether this knowledge will ever have practical relevance in our futures. Departing the auditorium, though, we enter the Walsh stoa, where a row of extremely tangible, colossal Ionic columns stretch two stories, their volutes winking down from above.

Sitting on the second floor of the Architecture Library in between classes, surrounded by a sliver of its impressive collection, we might read about ancient Greco-Roman temples. We glance up and see some of the same details just above us encouraged by a successful proposal of classical ornament in the 21st century. We glance down knowing that just below us is a unique and awe-inspiring collection of rare books dating all the way back to Leon Battista Alberti's *De Re Aedificatora* from 1485. Between the first published architectural treatise and our own future design philosophies we bookend the timeline of the classical world. Then, after absorbing the history of columns in *antis*, we pass between a real life example of such on the way to lunch.

The next day we take sketchbooks, pencils, and rulers in hand. We sit cross-legged on the Stoa floor, the columns squat and solid in front of us,

producing measured drawings of the profile of an Ionic base. Standing at a distance we are dwarfed by the monumental cylinders and try in vain to estimate how many feet tall they are. We venture outside to study windows and doors, back inside to replicate floor plans and ceiling plans, and up the twisting stair to plummet a measuring tape down to a classmate waiting below. Watching politely and silently in the background a bronze Alberti clutches antiquated editions of the same tools we still use centuries later.

His are not the only statuary eyes that can observe student exploration. The Hall of Casts, relocated from the original Bond Hall location, contains a Soane-ian assemblage of plaster statues and ornament in a skylit space. Sketchers sit themselves on the hall's floor, leaning against a replica of a Doric temple detail, sketchbooks on their knees, perhaps squinting up at a smaller-than-life Monument to Lysicrates. The silent

Right: Finger smearing on the page (Photo: Scenographia: Live-Drawing Event, 23-24 January, 2020).

space lulls them into an artistic fixation upon a soldier's foot, a chariot's wheel, or the curly beard of a reclining figure.

Such a building, even with the intention to prove to architecture students that contemporary classical designs can indeed come to fruition, could easily be stale. Walsh Family Hall is not. Its conjoined buildings, bright colors, and soaring spaces form an architectural playground. This is not to say that the hall is not also possessed of a certain grace; indeed it is that rare environment whose elegance seems neither stuffy nor forced. Perhaps the exemplifying feature of this sensation is the Alexandrian light tower with a beacon that beckons exhausted students warmly back to studio in the darkest hours of the night. Though not strictly necessary to the education of a class of architecture students, the tower gives Walsh Family Hall, and thus its students, faculty and staff, a charismatic presence and an atmosphere of quirky yet stately importance. Walsh is a place where, on a brief snack break from a long studio night, one is amused but not particularly surprised to see the colossal legs of a statue temporarily stored next to a vending machine.

These communal nights of seemingly interminable work are grueling and are at the core of the studio culture that every architecture student learns to cherish despite the exhaustion. A tall room with plenty of natural light, nooks for secret midday naps and a simultaneously industrial and homely character is key. The studio spaces in Walsh Family Hall enable the two most important pursuits of an architecture student: the design work itself and the familial community that emerges around it. For many on campus, studio is home.

As much as it encourages learning and growth from every corner Walsh Family Hall also understands the importance of both fun and serenity: of a chance to breathe. An exit to the terrace and the breeze that immediately hits is refreshing and revitalizing. This is where we take sandwich breaks, run laps to stay awake and remind ourselves what fresh air feels like. This is where we stomp out patterns in the winter snow, throw impeccably-designed paper airplanes in the fall and scare away birds in the spring. This is where we watch the sun set and, having stayed all night, watch the sun rise again.

Previous spread: The Stoa is used for many different activities and is designed so that it is overlooked from the café and from the studio spaces on the upper floor. This adds to the centrality of the Stoa to everyday student life at the School. (Photo: Scenographia: Live-Drawing Event, Walsh Family Hall, 23-24 January, 2020).

Right: Students enjoying the experience of studying rare Renaissance texts and engravings that the School has in its possession in the Ryan Rare Books Reading Room within the main Library.

Hallie Swenson

Dates of Study: 2017-2020, Notre Dame Class of 2020
Graduated with an M.Arch (Masters of Architecture)

Entering Walsh Family Hall, on the daily commute to the studio, the rich smell of Illy espresso comes wafting down from the cafe on the second level. The bright, elusive South Bend sun floods the Stoa creating sharp shadows and beautiful highlights on the massive Ionic columns. Sophomores can be found sitting around the column bases measuring the scotia, torus and plinth for their measured drawings. Laughter is heard from the fourth year students on the second floor as they reminisce about their favorite Roman gelateria. Walking up the grand staircase on the far end of the Stoa a group of fifth year students blocks the top of the stair while they debate the principles of New Urbanism and its importance in their designs. Entering the vast studio the sound of scratching pencils, animated conversations and rustling trace paper fills the air. Professors and students discuss their projects; changes that need to be made and deadlines that need to be met. Piles of books are found on every surface and a blanket of scratch paper keeps the desks warm from the Indiana winter. Innovation, imagination and creativity consume every bright young mind. This is Walsh Family Hall: our home and place of learning.

The School of Architecture students and staff moved from our beloved Bond Hall to the new Walsh Family Hall filled with curiosity and excitement. Not knowing what to expect each of us explored every room and marveled at the beauty found throughout the building. The serene beauty of the library contrasts the lively and colorful beauty in the Stoa; each exemplifying the variety that traditional architecture can offer. The studios, reaching long and wide, hold a maze of student desks. Each of us hang drawings on our desk dividers to make the space our own. The occasional indoor plant brings joy to those who pass by.

In the third floor studio the professors' offices line the length of the room. It is rare that a professor can make it to their office without stopping to comment on a student's work or a student stopping them to ask a question about the most recent assignment or exam. Each professor gladly engages in conversation and makes time for every student. It is common that small groups of students participate in a lengthy conversation with professors about topics not related to architecture at all. The professors are not just feeding us information to recite back to them; they teach us how to become curious about life, to learn from each other, care for each other and to become stewards of this earth. We discuss topics that broaden our scope of thinking and allow for a deeper comprehension of the human experience. Topics might include: the vastness of the cosmos, the importance of bees, the subtleties of non-verbal communication, and the best way to make a cup of coffee. These are the memories that make Walsh Family Hall special.

This exceptional experience found in Walsh Family Hall extends its teachings to Rome, Italy. Each student in the Notre Dame School of Architecture family has the opportunity to travel and live in the Eternal City. We see the origins of the classical language, the importance of urbanism, walkable cities, and the real meaning of durable materials. Learning from the past is forgotten in many other schools but it is knowledge from the past that enables us to make informed decisions about the future. We learn to sketch, watercolor and compose our ideas onto paper. We also learn how to live amongst a new community and a new culture, to understand the value of communication and adapting in difficult situations. We see the intricacies of architectural design and, above all, the importance of beauty. Rome is a teacher and we are all changed upon our return to South Bend. We notice the details and proportions that give life to classical architecture: some of which can be seen in Walsh Family Hall.

The new Walsh Family Hall has become our home and inspiration. The careful design and attention to detail give the students daily inspiration for the use of traditional architecture in our modern world. Students can study the proportion of the rooms, the variety of classical orders and the use of durable materials. It proves that classicism can be used to address modern functions while also emphasizing the importance of beauty. The building gives us encouragement for the future: that classical architecture is not a dying tradition but a thriving one. It gives us a glimpse of what our futures hold, the beauty that we can help bring to the built environment. The variety of column types, window openings and use of materials demonstrate the flexibility and meaning traditional architecture can portray. Classicism is not stagnant or tedious, it is expressive and vibrant. Walsh Family Hall is an exemplary traditional building that gives purpose to our architecture studies here at Notre Dame and a stepping stone for our careers.

Top: 2019 The Final Reviews taking place in the second floor studio space.

Following spread: The top floor studio space is utilitarian and practical but is also arranged with open ceilings so that students can learn how the structure of the roof and the servicing of the building work.

IV

THE
ÉCOLE DES
BEAUX-ARTS

John Simpson

A GREAT TEACHING TRADITION

The École des Beaux-Arts in Paris evolved the greatest system of architectural education ever devised. With origins in the French Royal Academy of Architecture established in 1671, it was reorganised as part of Napoleon's reforms to organisation; the name dates from the period of Napoleon III in 1863 when it achieved independence of the government.

Its original purpose was to re-establish architecture as a learned profession. In the Middle Ages architecture was part of the job of a master stone mason. The idea that it involved more than a knowledge of construction and structure and the detailed articulation of ornament was born out of the Renaissance. Whereas medieval construction was largely an iterative process where a cathedral could sometimes take a generation or more to build, the study of Ancient Roman Architecture rekindled an interest in the larger scale concepts such as the organisation of cities and required a wider appreciation of subjects such as philosophy, art, aesthetics and the classics. These skills in architecture were in the first instance largely developed in Italy and were passed on through long and laborious apprenticeships where pupils would learn from the master they served. It was only in France where on the King's initiative the education of Architects was organised and promoted at a national level. The result was formidable: it freed architects from the control of the guilds and set strict standards of competency and training encompassing a wide range of subjects within a system of education that subsequently became a model emulated virtually across the western world.

The École des Beaux-Arts established a recognised system of examination that students could follow in their pursuit of professional qualification. It set the standards, competence and the breadth of knowledge that students were expected to achieve and provided the libraries and the lectures in order to teach academic subjects such as mathematics, the classics, the history of architecture and philosophy. But as architecture also involves learning very practical skills the 'Atelier' system was devised to run in parallel. Students at various levels in their education were grouped together under the direction of a mentor or tutor, just as they would be in an office, so as to learn those skills of organisation, drawing, measurement and construction and to develop skills of how to deal with and persuade people and run an effective business, so as to be able to design and erect successful buildings.

Most importantly, however, the École des Beaux-Arts recognised that the central part of architectural education was not just the accumulation of relevant academic knowledge or simply developing skills at design and

Previous page: Salles des Études Antiques, École des Beaux-Arts. The Great Hall of Casts, equipped with an iron and glass roof, helped students to learn from classical examples. Study did not only include antique fragments, but also the French classical tradition.

Top right: École des Beaux-Arts, Paris, façade and forecourt.

Bottom right: Students in an atelier at the beginning of the 20th century.

PROMENADE
DU
NYMPHÉE

PLACE
DE LA
RÉPUBLIQUE

A. Vincent, 4 Rue des Beaux-Arts, Paris

drawing and the technicalities of how to put a building together, but learning how to manipulate the overall sculptural form of a building in relation to everything around it. Students needed to learn about scale, proportion and the role that mouldings and detail play in making this work. It is both a science and an art which is learned by experience and the study of other previous works. This is why at the centre of the École des Beaux-Arts there stood a vast Hall of Casts, and why architects like Soane collected endless fragments of Ancient buildings. Only by the study of these fragments can the sculptural aspects of architecture be understood together with the role that mouldings play in the visual articulation of a façade and fending off the elements away from the building so as to control the weathering of the materials, allowing the building to develop a patina which only improves its appearance as it grows old.

Many American architects attended the École des Beaux-Arts at the turn of the 20th century and some of the greatest architectural landmarks in the US – railroad stations, museums, Post Offices, the great government buildings in Washington D.C. – are the result.

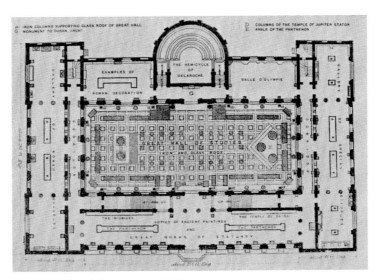

Left: Example of the work of students produced at the École des Beaux-Arts.

Above: École des Beaux-Arts, Paris: plan of the Palais des Études showing libraries and teaching spaces surrounding the Hall of Casts at the centre.

Left: The Hall of Casts at Walsh Family Hall provides architectural students at the University of Notre Dame with the opportunity to study the work of their predecessors and do so in a manner that was so successfully carried out at the École des Beaux-Arts in Paris in previous centuries. It is only through this careful study of casts and of fragments of old buildings that the sculptural aspects of architecture can be understood and for students to learn once more how to master the timeless language of classical architecture.

V

THE
ARCHITECTURE
OF
EDUCATION

John Simpson

INTRODUCTION

One thing that has always struck me about educational institutions is the way each has its own individual vision and unique way of doing things based on an ethic that usually goes back to its very origins and the principles of its founders. This observation has become strengthened as I have worked more closely over the years with different places of learning. What amazes me is how this ethic survives over decades and centuries and remains steadfast, despite the constant turnaround of personnel, teachers and academics and the annual throughput of students and pupils. It is astonishing how these institutions are able to do this generation after generation, and retain that distinctive quality that is unique to them. Some of the institutions I have worked with have had such unshakable confidence in their values and principles that they had no difficulty in responding to the ever-changing world around them without fear of loss or dilution. It is almost as if those values and traditions had become embedded in the very bricks and mortar of the place.

This is why I have found that educational establishments of all kinds value their buildings, most of the time preferring to retain rather than replace their stock. They are also on the whole very careful about adding new buildings, taking a long-term view mindful of the character of their estate. I have found that as an architect I have repeatedly been given commissions precisely because of the importance that John Simpson Architects as a practice places on architecture and tradition. The institutions that approach us are usually very attached and devoted to their buildings, despite having outgrown them. They come to us to explore how their buildings can be reconfigured so as to extend their life and enable them to fulfil the aspirations they have for the future.

Most have significantly larger numbers of staff, faculty and students from when they were first established. By the time we are involved as the architects, they have had several additions tacked on usually done on a piecemeal basis, over many years, in locations that may have seemed expedient at the time but have cumulatively had the effect of losing the clarity of organisation that once characterised the architecture of the original. Invariably the result involves the construction of new buildings, the removal of inappropriate previous additions and the reorganisation and modification of existing interiors so that the identity and the traditions that distinguish that particular institution from any other are retained.

Over the coming pages five examples are presented of the work of the practice. Four of them required us to work within established frameworks, two at the University of Cambridge, one at the University of Oxford and the fourth being the Royal College of Music, the leading conservatoire,

Previous page: The circular ceiling in the new stair hall at the Whittle Building at Peterhouse by John Simpson is decorated with radiating patterns of Gothic tracery in plasterwork and continues a tradition started at the College in the 1820s.

Right: View looking into the main Entrance Courtyard at the new Defence and National Rehabilitation Centre at Stanford Hall by John Simpson showing the Statue of Sir Robert Jones by the sculptor Alexander Stoddart that you see as you enter. It recalls the heroic work carried out in rehabilitation during the First World War.

in London (RCM). The Defence and National Rehabilitation Centre (DNRC) is a military rehabilitation centre where the intention in time is to add a civilian facility on the site so that research can be shared and for it to become the national teaching hospital in rehabilitation medicine. It has been located on an historic country house estate and incorporates architecture on the Estate that goes back to the 18th century. The work at these institutions provides the background and context for our approach to the design of the School of Architecture at Notre Dame, which occupies an entirely new site on the university campus.

First, the Oxford and Cambridge examples. Peterhouse is the oldest college at the University of Cambridge, whose buildings have evolved over more than seven hundred years. Gonville and Caius College is only slightly younger, having been founded as Gonville Hall in 1348 – the year of the Great Plague. Lady Margaret Hall, by contrast, was established only in the late-19th century but is distinguished as being the first college at either Oxford or Cambridge to be established with the specific purpose of educating women; it has a remarkable collection of 20th-century classical buildings. It is not surprising that the achievements and traditions of these colleges have come to be symbolised by the buildings that they inhabit. Their form follows the model of monastic cloisters around courts or quadrangles that the older colleges derive from and where the idea of a sanctuary for learning originates.

After the fall of the Roman Empire civilization survived in abbeys and monasteries. These self-sufficient, closed communities provided sanctuary from an otherwise hostile world; they became the centres of charity, for the healing of the sick, for contemplation and for teaching and learning. We do not only see this heritage at ancient universities like at Oxford and Cambridge; it became the tradition of many more modern universities built in the nineteenth and twentieth centuries, in particular in the US. The architecture of university campuses, such as at the University of Notre Dame, makes the association with medieval sanctuaries of learning through the Collegiate Gothic detailing of their buildings.

In their heyday, abbeys and monasteries would have been some of the most imposing and most architectural structures that existed. Their built form would have represented the values of the communities to which these buildings belonged and the activities that they were connected with. Cloisters and quadrangles became the form of buildings connected with learning.

Structure was important to the religious life, including study. For example, Cistercian Abbeys regardless of their location and the materials that they were built of bear a recognisable architecture and organisation. They were built by the order strictly to follow the model of the mother Abbey at Citeaux near Dijon which was created to embody the values and principles of the order as espoused by St Benedict. Despite the austerity of monastic life, the Cistercians were practical organisers who constantly added to their buildings. They strove to create a utopian foretaste of the Heavenly Jerusalem that awaited in the next world. Their achievements have a very seductive architectural dimension.

By the time of the Renaissance the connection between learning and a monastic environment was well and truly established. So, when Cosimo de Medici set up the Medici Academy in Florence in 1437, he did so in a former monastery, the Convent of San Marco. With the help of the architect Michelozzo, he rebuilt the convent around two cloisters, embellished the chapel with works by Fra Angelico and Fra Bartolomeo and built the Laurentian library to house Niccolò di Niccoli's collection of manuscripts that Cosimo and later his grandson Lorenzo supplemented with a further precious collection of books and rare Greek and Latin texts retrieved following the fall of Constantinople. In Lorenzo the Magnificent's day the Academy became the engine for promoting Renaissance thought throughout Europe with philosophers like Marsilio Ficino, Polziano, and Pico della Mirandola and artists like Sandro Botticelli, Leonardo Da Vinci and Michelangelo Buonarroti, merging Humanist and Christian religious thought.

Right: Stone arched window recalls a screen that once existed on the site of the Whittle Building, Peterhouse, Cambridge.

104

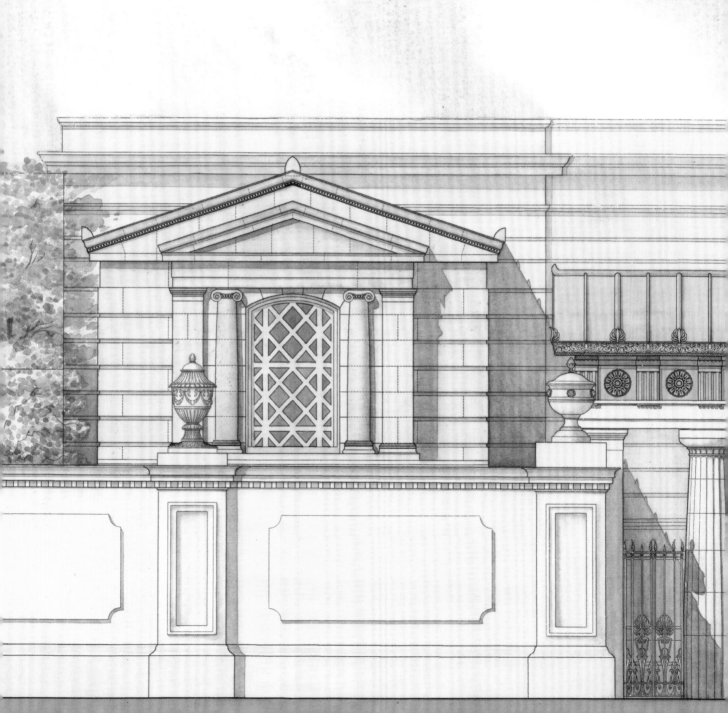

From then the idea of Plato's Academy and the Christian monastic cloister or quadrangle are forever architecturally intertwined as an expression of the world of academia. The Renaissance tradition is important in that an understanding of art and architecture becomes a significant aspect of a liberal arts education. It was regarded as important as philosophy, the classics, literature and mathematics. The difference with architecture is that it is not something that can be learned simply from books. It is three dimensional, involving issues of scale, proportion and form and is a response to the location it is in and its surroundings. Theoretical study is not enough; it can only be appreciated properly through the experience of standing next to it, feeling it and walking through it. Which is why those able to afford it embarked on the Grand Tour as an important part of their overall education. Some brought back paintings and engravings from the Grand Tour, others returned home to recreate some of that experience for others, unable to travel, to learn from and enjoy by incorporating references and details of what they saw into their buildings. Dr Caius who was a major benefactor for his college and later became master of Gonville and Caius, at Cambridge sought to do just this after returning from his studies at Padua University. He set out to make architecture too part of his students' experience and education at Gonville and Caius. Many of the buildings at Oxford and Cambridge followed the example of Cosimo de Medici in Florence, using their very architecture as a means of celebrating the Ancient and Renaissance worlds of Italy. The intention was to disseminate the Humanist ideals of antiquity and educate the young so as to serve a new enlightened world.

When we designed the portico at the Queen's Gallery at Buckingham Palace, we had the opportunity to do something similar to prepare people visiting the Royal Collection to help them enjoy and make the most out of their visit. The architecture deliberately reminds visitors of the origins of western architecture. It makes the architecture of the new gallery an interactive, enjoyable and educational part of the visitors' experience. At Eton College, our choice of references and details incorporated into McCrum Yard serve a comparable purpose. They allow the pupils at Eton to experience elements from Greek, Roman and Hellenistic architecture connected with the school's fine collection of antiquities from the ancient world which is housed in the museum building within the scheme. The references and forms within the debating chamber also give a glimpse into the origins of western democracy that the pupils study at the School of Politics and Economics, also located in an adjacent building in the new quadrangle. In addition, interested students can rejoice as they learn by exploring the references, so that the very architecture of the new School buildings is a liberal education in itself. Even the fountain serves as a practical teaching tool reminding pupils of the importance of renewable energy so that the pupils experience of the architecture is an integral part of the teaching at the school.

The DNRC is both a teaching hospital for rehabilitation medicine as well as a place of healing. Like schools and universities, hospitals and

Previous spread: The Portico and the Entrance Hall at the Queen's Gallery at Buckingham Palace, designed by John Simpson, reference the origins of Western Art and Architecture and employ the archaic Doric orders from the temples at Paestum. The open pediment to the portico recalls the traditional origin of the Greek Doric in timber as claimed in the ancient texts by Vitruvius and in the entrance Hall sculpture by Alexander Stoddart celebrates the reign of HM Queen Elizabeth II through allegorical scenes from Homer's *Iliad* and *Odyssey*, the first works of art in Western literature.

Left: The Gate of Honour in Caius Court. Dr Caius designed and built three gates in the 1560s to signal the different stages of academic life. Students pass through the Gate of Humility upon matriculation, as they enter the college, the Gate of Virtue while students and the Gate of Honour as they leave as Graduates.

sanatoria as building forms derive directly from the monastic tradition. It was therefore easy to settle on a building form that would create an environment that serves both the mental and physical wellbeing of its users, which meant in this case being conducive to the rehabilitation of patients and as a place of learning for the teaching of medicine. It is based around a series of arcaded courts, gardens and cloisters.

At the RCM, the buildings are again planned around a quadrangle that provides the space around which all the public functions of the conservatoire are centred. This both responds to the educational use of the building and the context provided by the existing buildings and the tall Italianate tower originally built for the Imperial Institute which can be seen from the new court.

The Walsh Family Hall School of Architecture by contrast is designed on a completely new site. This provides the opportunity to create the ideal building configuration to enable students to obtain an education in comfortable and attractive surroundings and also to learn about architecture through the building itself. The Notre Dame School, too, already has an established teaching tradition derived from the École des Beaux-Arts in Paris which had such an influence on American

Top: The pediment of the portico at the Queen's Gallery at Buckingham Palace is crowned with an acroterion of enormous size and dynamism recalling that at the temple of Artemis at Magnesia on the Meander of 150BC by Hermogenes of Priene, a favourite architect of Vitruvius.

architects at the turn of the 20th century and produced numerous splendid railroad stations, museums, government buildings and other architectural landmarks in the United States.

The new School is designed as an Academy comprising of a number of buildings which together form a court deriving from Plato's garden, the cloister as a monastic sanctuary and the Renaissance place of learning with its library. It picks up on the Beaux-Arts academy too with its hall of casts and atelier system. The range of buildings serve also as a teaching tool each showing the different priorities needed in order to design buildings of various types. Unusually it has at its centre a stoa, a building type once at the heart of every ancient Greek city. They provided a covered public meeting place where merchants sold their goods and public meetings happened. The Greek philosopher Zeno gave his founding lectures in the Stoa Poikile in Athens. Stoae were the symbol of community. It is highly appropriate, therefore, to a School of Architecture today where a major preoccupation of the 21st century is going to be to address the issues associated with a burgeoning world urban population and the creation of appropriate cities that foster community and are agreeable and enjoyable places in which to live. This Stoa at the heart of Walsh Family Hall addresses the priorities of the age and architecturally gives scale to the buildings and shows how the Orders can be used together in unison.

There are glimpses too of the recent Modern era in the Stoa and you are reminded of the work of architects such as James Sterling by the way it is incorporated into the overall composition, and the Alexandrine lighthouse, as a beacon of learning, is a reminder of Leon Krier evoking the School's urbanist credentials.

Architecture is an important element of our existence as human beings. It shapes our experience as we wander around and through the buildings we share with our neighbours and friends. This common experience is what binds us together and is an important factor that contributes to the identity of the community to which we belong. Even though we may not realise it, it is perhaps the most significant part of our education and culture that we pass on to our children and grandchildren as they are growing up.

McCRUM YARD, ETON COLLEGE

McCrum Yard was, according to the Provost of Eton College, Lord Waldergrave, the 'last great site' that Eton could develop. It has done so with a scheme by John Simpson that is both elegant and erudite, providing a debating chamber – the Jafar Hall – that is influenced by the Council Chamber known as the Ekklesiasterion at Priene, now in Turkey. Classrooms serve both God (theology) and Mammon (economics), as well as modern languages and politics. One Order derives from Miletus, an impure combination of Corinthian and Ionic elements, whose capital includes palm leaves. Being only used outside Greece, it was deemed appropriate for a building devoted to the teaching of languages and studies of other cultures.

There is also a state-of-the-art museum, the Jafar Gallery to display the internationally important collection of antiquities that Eton was given by a former member of the college at the end of the 19th century. Mahogany cabinets contain a coffin, mummified heads, Egyptian blue faience, votive feet and trays of coins. There are Greek vases that belonged to Sir William Hamilton, husband of Nelson's beloved Emma. Previously too fragile to put on show in the inadequate conditions available to the college, the collection can now be visited by the public through an entrance to the outside world: a space that also takes the form of a small outdoor theatre.

The Jafar Hall Debating Chamber has a particular value for a school that has produced many prime ministers. 'We believe in debating,' says Lord Waldegrave. 'Above all we believe in people being taught to speak properly.' The hall takes its name from the Eton-educated United Arab Emirates family who sponsored the £18.2 million project. Microphones are deliberately absent from the chamber to encourage boys to project their voices naturally and to command a chamber as if it might be the House of Commons, although the colour of the red leather benches is that of the House of Lords.

Much of the craftsmanship is British. The immense two hundred and seventy-six pound copper acroterion above the museum was made in Cornwall. Michael Johnson, one of the coppersmiths responsible, calls it 'one of the most complex and intricate pieces of handcrafted architectural copperwork made in this country in a generation.' The stone carving took place in Wiltshire, the joinery in Suffolk and the huge doors were made in Oxford. McCrum Yard is named after the late headmaster Michael McCrum. The site was previously occupied by an impractical 1970s structure. Being visible from Windsor Castle gave it a particular sensitivity.

Left: A giant vaulted archway forms the entrance to the new quadrangle at Eton College as you enter from Keate's Lane.

Following spread: The new McCrum Yard, looking towards the new Museum and Debating Chamber. A fountain forms the centrepiece to the quadrangle which provides cooling for the hall within using a process of evaporative cooling.

Bottom left: The arcade at the Birley School of modern languages features capitals based on an original order from Asia Minor and was considered appropriate to a school of foreign languages, McCrum Yard, Eton College, Windsor.

Bottom right: The route into McCrum Yard from the School features a triumphal arch. This Arch provides a link between the buildings that form the new quadrangle connecting the departments at the upper levels.

Top left: The design of the Debating Chamber is inspired by that of the Ekklesasterion which is the Council Chamber in Ancient Priene in Asia Minor and recalls the origins of Western Democracy.

Above: The new display cabinets in the Museum provide security and the necessary environmental conditions for the conservation of the College's ancient Egyptian and classical antiquities allowing the space to be double used as a breakout space for the adjacent Debating Chamber.

Above: Plan of the new academic quadrangle at Eton College formed by the buildings for the departments of Modern Languages, Philosophy and Divinity, and Politics and Economics. The centrepiece is a new Debating Chamber and Museum.

Site Plan:
1. Jafar Hall 2. Jafar Gallery
3. Lyttelton & Elliot Schools 4. Birley School

Top right: The Entrance to the Museum from Keate's Lane is through two loggias that form an external amphitheatre off the street.

Bottom right: The entrance from within McCrum Yard is detailed so as to provide a foretaste of the antiquities that are contained within.

LADY MARGARET HALL, UNIVERSITY OF OXFORD

It has been said that under the founder and first principal, Elizabeth Wordsworth, Lady Margaret Hall (LMH) students were as 'daughters at home with a unique, original and much respected mother who knew everyone worth knowing.' This describes the situation of the College as it was in the nineteenth and the early part of the twentieth centuries. While there were only nine students at LMH when it was founded in 1879, today, with over 400 undergraduates and 150 graduate students, the College is a different institution. It was granted full college status in 1962, and has, since 1979, admitted men as well as women.

In the Northern suburbs of Oxford LMH was well provided with land when it was founded, but much of the site was unsuitable for building. Sir Reginald Blomfield designed student accommodation, library and dining hall, with a Wren-like centrepiece and a semi-circular portico reminiscent of Bramante's Tempietto in Rome. Sir Giles Gilbert Scott added the chapel, more accommodation, an enlarged dining hall and common room facilities. In the 1960s Raymond Erith added a new library building and built an austere brick range in front of the college entrance to form a quad, cleverly designed to provide a view through the main entrance arch that makes use of Blomfield's semi-circular portico. The range also makes reference to Rome's Porta Maggiore. After Erith's time two high-rise blocks were constructed to provide accommodation, disrupting the quad pattern that was developing and had probably been in mind from the beginning.

John Simpson restored the quadrangular form of the college by adding new undergraduate and graduate accommodation and teaching rooms to create quads that integrate the free-standing tower blocks into the architecture of the college. Although distinguished, Erith's work was too severe to be popular; Simpson built in front of it two new ranges together with two Doric gatehouses linked by a grille that also has the effect of creating another new quad that encloses the space. The architecture ingeniously makes reference to the tomb of Eurysaces the Baker which stands next to the Porta Maggiore in Rome, to form a dialogue with Erith's erudite composition.

Left: The undergraduate teaching and residential accommodation of the Pipe Partridge Building form a new arcaded quad within the College.

Following spread: The new three sided entrance quad to the College softens the austere quality of Erith's entrance to the College and through the detailing of the Gate Pavilions builds up an architectural dialogue with Erith's building.

Above: The Hall within the Clore Graduate Centre which is one of the buildings that form the new front quad to LMH.

Right: Interior of the new Porters' Lodge is part of the new Donald Fothergill graduate building that forms the other side of the new front quad.

Previous spread: The new Simpkins Lee Lecture Hall is designed
so that the acoustics can be varied to also work as a recital room
for music and a theatre for drama. The extraction vents are hidden
behind the paterae at the corners of the dome.

Above: The new buildings added to LMH are shown in dark grey and
incorporate inappropriately sited buildings into the quadrangular
development structure of the College.

Right: The unusual design of the architectural embellishment of the
pediments of the gate Pavilions is a reference to the ancient Roman
tomb by the Porta Maggiore in Rome of the baker Eurysaces.

GONVILLE & CAIUS, UNIVERSITY OF CAMBRIDGE

In 1993, John Simpson won a competition to remodel the main historic heart of the college at Gonville and Caius College. The project followed the acquisition of C. R. Cockerell's neo-Classical masterpiece – originally one wing of his incomplete scheme for a University Library, more recently in use as a law library – which stands next to the college by the Gate of Honour. This was transformed into a new library for the college which in turn made two large rooms previously used as the college library available for other purposes. This provided the opportunity for Simpson to rework and remodel some of the oldest parts of the college in Gonville Court as well as the hall and kitchens built by Anthony Salvin in the 19th century, creating the bar, student and fellows' combination rooms, seminar and teaching rooms and new student accommodation on the top floor. A new building was also constructed in the kitchen court providing new service spaces and a new elevator to bring the facilities in line with modern standards.

A significant element within the project involved the remodelling of the two large spaces, previously the library, for the use of the fellows. One of these rooms had formed part of the historic college hall built in the 1400s and remodelled by Sir John Soane in 1792. Despite Soane's scheme being destroyed in the 19th century when Salvin built the new hall and the old hall was subdivided into rooms, Simpson felt it would be possible to recreate a version of it. The new Lord Colyton Hall (named after the donor) could never have been a literal copy however because not all of the original details are known; for one thing the room is smaller as Salvin had altered the proportions by raising the floor. Also the needs of modern conservation practice meant that the new decoration could not be permanently attached to the medieval fabric within which it is set.

The result evokes the ingenuity and drama associated with Soane that Simpson understands so well. A relatively small space is given a monumental character by a barrel-vaulted roof coffered in the spirit of the Baths of Ancient Rome. Towards the end of the room is a large arch cum screen containing seven circular openings or oculi, a motif that Soane borrowed from Bramante in Milan and first used in the library at Wimpole Hall. Behind the oculi is a window of amber glass creating a sensation of mystery and warmth that reflects Soane's genius in the manipulation of light as seen, for example, in his own house in Lincoln's Inn Fields in London. The second library space was transformed into a new dining room for the fellows.

Left: The new Fellows' Dining Room was created out of Salvin's old library. The new interior references Cockrell's building where the library was moved to by using the order from the temple of Apollo at Bassae to design the new interior.

Top: Section through the West Range of Gonville Court showing the new building (shown coloured yellow) inserted into the kitchen court to provide additional kitchens, pantries, serveries, WCs and services as well as a new elevator shaft.

Bottom: The long table in the Fellows' Dining Room is designed to work as several freestanding components with klismos chairs that can be stacked.

Above: The new staircase leading from the bar area to the students' common room.

When the late Professor David Watkin described the Fellows' Dining Room at Gonville and Caius College, Cambridge he wrote: 'Simpson has here achieved what is without doubt one of the most inventive, ornamental, yet scholarly classical interiors created in England for many years.' Writing in *The Buildings of England* volume for Cambridgeshire, the architectural historian went further; he described the effect of the Greek detail as having 'a hallucinatory quality'. The effect comes from the recreation of the cella or sacred room of the Temple of Apollo Epicurius at Bassae with its attached Ionic order and distinctive capitals of curving volutes. Erudition is appropriate in a college setting and the reference to Bassae doubly so here: the temple was excavated by the architect C. R. Cockerell who incorporated the order into his plans for the University Library, next to Gonville and Caius, only one wing of which was built. One of the unique features of the Bassae temple is the carved frieze which runs around the inside of the cella; it is now in the British Museum. In the Fellows' Dining Room, Simpson reproduces it between the windows. The sumptuous colours of the room reflect the polychromy that would have decorated the original.

Left: The new roof lit servery for the refurbished Dining Hall built within the old kitchen court at Gonville and Caius College, Cambridge.

Right: The Dining Hall designed by Anthony Salvin in 1853 refurbished with new panelling and joinery to the gallery and the screens passage.

Above: The new Lord Colyton Room created from the
old Munro library based on a design by John Soane for
the Dining Hall in Gonville Court.

Top: Watercolour of Soane's 1792 design for the
Dining Hall in Gonville Court.. The new Lord Colyton
Room was based on Soane's design for the room.

Bottom: View of the new Bar area which is part of
the new social facilities designed for the students at
the College.

THE WHITTLE BUILDING, PETERHOUSE, UNIVERSITY OF CAMBRIDGE

Peterhouse is the oldest college in Cambridge, founded in 1286. Behind Old Court is a relative newcomer, Gisborne Court, built in the 1820s in a Tudor Gothic style by the otherwise little-known William McIntosh Brooks. This three-sided court was initially closed by a screen that was replaced in the 1930s by a single-storey, brick bathhouse named after the then Master, Field-Marshal William Birdwood. One night in the summer of 1977 a group of students performed an egregious act of vandalism on the Birdwood Building, by moving all the bathtubs onto the lawn. This was to force the college authorities to redevelop the site for a new undergraduate common room. The campaign failed at the time; forty years later, however, the need to replace the defunct Birdwood was recognised.

John Simpson was commissioned to develop a masterplan for the historic heart of the college, which resolved the inefficiencies that had crept in over the years and provided a new service entrance (no mean feat given the sensitivities of this ancient site). The centrepiece of this scheme is the Whittle Building in Gisborne Court, named after Frank Whittle, the Petrean who invented the jet engine. This provided a new junior common room, twenty-two student rooms, a gym, a function room, two music practice rooms, a guest room and a set or suite for one of the college fellows.

Cambridge has a more open and Picturesque character than Oxford and courts built around three sides, with a screen closing the fourth side, are often found; the most conspicuous example is at King's College where the Gothic screen and gatehouse were designed by the mathematician and architect William Wilkins, better known as a Greek Revivalist. Old Court at Peterhouse is also three-sided; the centre of the fourth side is occupied by the chapel which was built in the mid-17th century in the Gothic style promoted by Archbishop Laud in deference to the Medieval surroundings. Today the ancient rubblestone walls of Old Court are not seen because they were refaced in the Georgian period to present a unified facade; but they still exist beneath the 18th century ashlar. The Medieval buildings that faced Gisborne Court were also refaced to match William McIntosh Brooks's buildings unifying the court just as had been done a century beforehand in Old Court.

Left: The Whittle building echoes the Gothic style of Gisborne Court started by McIntosh Brooks in 1825 maintaining the Peterhouse tradition of architecturally uniform Courts.

Previous spread: The design of the Whittle Building has an arcade, which references a Gothic screen that once stood on the site and was demolished in 1939. The new Junior Combination Room breaks through the arcade in the manner of the Peterhouse Chapel in the adjacent Old Court.

This page: A new stair hall has been introduced with a staircase wrapping around a Doric column leading to the new bar, gym and function room at basement level of the adjacent refurbished Fen Court building designed in 1939 by Hughes and Bicknell.

Architecturally, the details such as window mouldings, architraves and skirtings continue the theme of a unified court so characteristic of Peterhouse, but Simpson's building is both more accomplished and made of better materials. At the heart of the triangular plan is a circular staircase which rises through the full three storeys. A second staircase curves around a giant Doric column. This staircase is itself set in a curving window bay which echoes the form of a nearby Modernist building from shortly before the Second World War, Fen Court, which was renovated as part of the scheme.

Right: A circular stone cantilevered stair rises to all three levels of the building and reconciles the geometry of the building which is on a triangular site. The top floor of the stair hall accommodates a circular shaped study in the fellow's set with spectacular views across Coe Fen.

Following spread: The rear of the Whittle building as seen from Coe Fen showing the service ramp under the building leading to the college kitchens.

THE DEFENCE AND NATIONAL REHABILITATION CENTRE, LOUGHBOROUGH

The new Defence and National Rehabilitation Centre, on the Stanford Hall estate outside Loughborough, is remarkable on many levels. Medically, it represents an outstanding resource to help wounded service personnel recover from their injuries and trauma, some of which are horrific. The Armed Forces have an outstanding record in putting their wounded back, quite literally in some cases, on their feet; their success far outstrips that of the National Health Service (NHS). The intention is that the state-of-the-art equipment at the DNRC will in due course be shared with the NHS so that it can become the major teaching hospital for rehabilitation medicine in the country, hence the reference to 'National' in the title.

The architecture is no less exceptional. Patients would, it is believed, thrive best in an atmosphere of ordered calm and familiarity. The Duke of Westminster, who paid for the building, was firm in his belief that this could only be achieved through classicism. In addition to that, ample evidence was emerging from research in neuroscience that in order to activate the immune system in patients a tranquil and reassuring environment was essential. It was felt that a classical scheme would unconsciously evoke a tradition of military architecture with which the patients would be instinctively comfortable. What we have, therefore, is both a public building which is classical, probably the first for half a century, and the greatest extent of brickwork laid in one project since the Second World War.

Clearly the Grade II★ listed historic landmark building on site was not suited to conversion to intensive clinical use. On the other hand, a country house with the usual ancillary buildings provides a good model on which to organise a complex project such as the DNRC and in which to provide the associated teaching and research facilities required. With the different clinical and sports facilities that needed to be housed, along with messes, bars and several types of accommodation, the brief was involved; it required around 400,000 square feet of floor space. The country house-and-outbuildings model meant that it could be achieved without becoming overwhelmingly institutional. The human scale has been preserved. This together with the architecture of enclosed courtyards and cloistered gardens that draws its influence from the monastic infirmaries makes the DNRC feel friendly, rather than threatening. It provides a sense of enclosure and provides relative sanctuary from the outside world. The Picturesque approach also

Left: View looking into the arcaded main entrance court. This is a practical space as well as a garden to enjoy with steps, ramps, and different floor finishes incorporated into the design for amputees to practice using their new prosthetic limbs.

provides maximum flexibility, allowing more space to be added piecemeal as and when needed: an important requirement for the military who cannot predict the nature of future conflicts.

The old house is now framed by two new blocks to disguise its length which was increased by the addition of a new wing to balance a large existing theatre built by a previous owner. The ends of these blocks have Diocletian windows to the upper floor while the windows of the long facades are set in recessed arcades. Any severity is leavened by the rosy colour of the brick. Elsewhere, important buildings are distinguished by the use of yellow brick; while this adds variation, it was also a necessary response to obtaining enough brick given the very large demand made by this project.

The hospital facilities are organised around courts landscaped with paths with different surface textures – uneven concrete, pebbles – allowing patients to practice the use of prosthetic limbs. Elsewhere, courtyard gardens have been designed with steps of different height for the same purpose.

Top: Specialised facilities are treated as individual landmarks to help patients orientate themselves, much as a chapel would in a college setting.

Bottom: Different parts of the DNRC have an individual character so that patients discover a place to find tranquillity and contentment.

Right: Timber colonade at the DNRC. Drawing on monastic and collegiate models, the buildings form garden courts, cloisters and arcaded quadrangles to link large and small buildings together.

Previous spread: The entrance building to the Clinical Core. It takes the form of a coach house so as to maintain a relationship which is in scale with the historic building, Stanford Hall, and is sensitive to its setting.

Right: The main entrance court contains a statue of Major General Sir Robert Jones and a frieze depicting the work of the DNRC by the sculptor Alexander Stoddart. Sir Robert Jones was head of the Medical Corps, was active during the First World War and is considered the father of Rehabilitation Medicine in Britain.

MAJOR GENERAL SIR ROBERT JONES Bt KBE CB TD FRS
1857–1933

ROYAL COLLEGE OF MUSIC, LONDON

The Royal College of Music is the No 1 Conservatoire for the Performing Arts in the UK (according to the QS World University Rankings 2016-2020). John Simpson's task in reimagining its campus, opposite the Royal Albert Hall in London, has not only created an inspirational learning environment for the great composers and artists of the future, but will boost the experience of the tens of thousands of musicians and concertgoers who visit each year.

The new development is centred on an open court arranged at the heart of the RCM's complex of new and existing buildings which together with the RCM's purchase of RCM Jay Mews, formerly the home of English National Ballet, have nearly doubled the capacity of the campus. This has delivered two new technically advanced performance spaces, additional rehearsal and practice rooms, world-class recording and digital facilities, and a spectacular new Royal College of Music Museum to showcase and increase public access to its internationally significant collections of historic musical instruments, artefacts and music-related art. There is also a beautifully restored and enlarged entrance hall, a large new public café, and a triple-height atrium that has the effect of visually reconnecting the public spaces within the College with the Royal Albert Hall opposite. It also has the effect of transforming the circulation system by introducing new pathways connecting the RCM's new and existing performance spaces. The College will now accommodate greater public participation and involvement, while offering the highest quality teaching environment, equipped with the latest technology.

Further substantial investment in technology has ensured students have access to state-of-the-art facilities and enables millions around the world to engage with the RCM's work through continuing digitisation of its collections, streaming and recording of performances, as well as enhancing and developing new ways of learning and performing. The increased physical capacity of the building will also transform the College's public engagement programme, allowing more people than ever to connect with the RCM in a variety of ways.

Both of the RCM's new performance spaces have been designed and constructed with the highest quality music-making in mind. They are completely acoustically isolated from the rest of the building, using 'box-in-a-box' construction, and can vary their acoustic properties so that they can be readily adapted for different types of musical performances and events. They have advanced air-handling and climate-control, enabling performances on the delicate instruments from the Royal College of

Left: The Royal College of Music's £40 million transformation, which centres on an open internal court built alongside the renowned Amaryllis Fleming Concert Hall and behind the Blomfield Building, forms the heart of RCM's new reworked Campus located opposite the Royal Albert Hall. Together with RCM's Jay Mews, formerly the home of English National Ballet this expansion has nearly doubled the capacity and opens up the College to greater public participation and involvement taking the College well into the 21st century.

Right: The new facilities around a soaring triple-height foyer provide two new performance spaces, a new museum, recording facilities, practice rooms, new student and public dining and cafe areas as well as the new circulation spaces, elevators, toilets and kitchens required. It creates an inspirational learning environment to serve the great composers and artists of the future as well as provide an enjoyable experience for tens of thousands of musicians and concerts-goers who visit the RCM each year.

Music Museum's collection. Both venues incorporate flexible capabilities for lighting, recording, streaming, projection and public performance. All the acoustic devices and technology have been efficiently incorporated within the design to create an elegant space for students and public alike. The new Royal College of Music Museum – with more than 15,000 musical treasures, including the earliest known guitar, the earliest stringed keyboard instrument and the most recognised portraits of Joseph Haydn and Farinelli – will place the collections in the heart of the new-look RCM, providing excellent public access for the first time.

Top right: View looking up to the glass roof over the spectacular new top lit internal foyer spaces, which together with an open court at ground floor form the heart of the new Royal College of Music. These new public spaces link together the new and existing facilities of the School so as to enable students and the public to share in the heritage of this remarkable institution, enjoy its music making and appreciate its new museum and library as well as the architecture of its buildings.

Bottom right: Watercolour by Chis Draper showing the new court at the Royal College of Music with the view of the Italianate tower built for the Imperial Institute behind. Below the court are two new recital and performance spaces and a new museum housing the College's collection of historic instruments.

Left: The new state-of-the-art Recital Hall at RCM has been acoustically engineered to provide a space with the flexibility suitable for the performance of a wide range of different types of music. It is also designed using 'box within a box' technology so that it can be used for recording and streaming music designed to reach wider world wide audiences.

Following spread: Behind the front facade of Arthur Blomfield's Royal College of Music in Kensington, the Main Entrance Hall has been enlarged to link with the new court, foyer and facilities. The objective is to make music at the RCM accessible to a wider public and relate more directly to the Royal Albert Hall opposite.

'The Tradition we call Architecture goes back to the beginning of time. The way we have built in the past has influenced us and our ancestors and has evolved slowly over generations. It draws on what everyone knows from the past and is the means by which we co-operate in building a shared environment for the future. This way we create new buildings that remind us of all the other the places that we love and enjoy. Like any tradition it continues to be an iterative process and remains one of the most dynamic cultural phenomena the world has ever seen, as contemporary as the generation interpreting it is imaginative.'

John Simpson of John Simpson Architects

ACKNOWLEDGEMENTS

John Simpson

First of all, we would like to thank the Walsh Family without whom this project would never have become a reality, in particular Matt and Joyce not only for their outstanding generosity but also for all the interest and encouragement that they provided us throughout the project. In addition to that we owe thanks to Carolyn and Robert Turner, Michael and Pearl Chesser, John and Weiqing Torti, David Manfredi and Elizabeth Lowrey, and Mark Wight and Ezster Borvendeg without whose contribution we would not have been able to provide many of those important features that have made the buildings so special as a School of Architecture. We would also like to thank the University and the trustees and especially Joe O'Neill and former executive Vice President John Affleck Graves both of whom provided continual support for the project throughout the development of the scheme. To the Dean Michael Lykoudis, the Advisory Council to the School and the Building Committee who together with Doug Marsh of the University Architects Department have been such a wonderful and inspiring client to work with. To the Faculty of the School for providing constructive criticism without ever overstepping the mark and curbing that instinctive temptation every architect has: to pick up a pencil and design the building themselves. To the many people in the faculty too who worked so hard to provide all the information essential for a good design, John Stamper on the detail of the brief, Jennifer Parker on the Library, Bob Brandt on the workshops and for the boundless energy that Craig Tiller, Shay Nothstine, Jamie LaCourt and Barbara Panzica put in to making sure everything is as it should be. Also, to Mary Beth Zachariades for making sure that we never unintentionally trod on anyone's toes.

I would also like to thank our US associates led by William Ketcham of Stantec for all the patience and hard work and good humour that he and his team put in make this project a reality and to Christopher Derrick of the ICCA Chicago Midwest Chapter for introducing me to him. To the team, Robert Tazelaar, Aaron Tabares and Declan Walsh of Arup who worked on the services design, Peter Schaudt (1959-2015) and Stan Szwalek of Hoerr Schaudt for the landscape and Donald Hamilin and Julia Seitchik of Thornton Tomasetti for the design of the structure, for providing such a formidable and efficient technical team and to Sean Walsh and Lou Rosetti of Walsh Construction for organising and ensuring that the building was built efficiently with accuracy and precision to the high standards that we and the University were looking for and especially to Aaron Holy of Walsh Construction who put tireless effort into making everything happen on site.

To the subcontractors Bybee Stone for the stonework carving, Ateliers Perrault for the joinery of the stoa stair, and the sculptor Sandy Stoddart for his remarkable statue of Leon Battista Alberti.

Finally I would like to thank my co-director Joanna Wachowiak and Tiffany Abernathy, the project director in day to day charge of the project with her team of Notre Dame Alumni Eamon Murphy, Fernando Gandara and Rena Multaputri whose boundless energy did not seem to recognise any time constraint: the working day seemed to merge, starting in the morning in London and not finishing until the office in Chicago went to sleep!

Michael Lykoudis

We are indebted to the university for allowing us to build in such a prominent site, to Fr. John I. Jenkins CSC, Provost Tom Burish, and former executive Vice President John Affleck Graves. We are also grateful to our principal benefactors Matthew and Joyce Walsh. Also to Carolyn and Robert Turner, Michael and Pearl Chesser, John and Weiqing Torti, and David Manfredi and Elizabeth Lowrey.

I would like to thank my colleagues on the School's building committee: Aimee Buccellato, Alan DeFrees, Richard Economakis, Jennifer Hoover, Barbara Panzica, Jennifer Parker (Hesburgh Libraries) John Stamper and Samir Younes. From the University Architects office, Doug Marsh, Craig Tiller and Shay Nothstine.

Finally to the Architects: From John Simpson Architects: to John Simpson, Joanna Wachowiak, and Tiffany Abernathy. From VOA now Stantec: to William Ketcham, Andrzej Mordzinski, Marie Kruse, Siobhan Mooney, and Gayle Soberg.

Building Donors

The Walsh Family Hall was made possible by generous donations from:

Matthew & Joyce Walsh – Walsh Family Hall
Lead Building Donors

Charles & Mary Lee Sheftic – Sheftic Family Alumni Plaza
Michael & Pearl Chesser – Chesser Family Tower
Bob & Carolyn Turner – Turner Family Hall of Casts
David Manfredi & Elizabeth Lowrey – Domenic & Elsie Manfredi Auditorium
John Torti & Weiqing Feng – Torti Family Stoa
Kevin & Mary Mulhall – Mulhall Family Exhibition Hall
Tim & Theresa Korth – Timothy W. & Theresa S. Korth Dean's Suite
Timothy & Donna Panzica – Tim & Donna Panzica Classroom
Mark Wight & Eszter Borvendeg
Michael & Leah Ryan – Ryan Companies Furniture Studio
James & Louise Nolan – Nolen Family Digital Design Studio
Bob & Kathy Snyder – Thomas Gordon Smith Seminar Room
Susan, Jill & Bradley Van Auken – Richard A. Van Auken '57 & Family Seminar Room
Ronald Blitch – James & Hilda Blitch Seminar Room
Andrew & Mary Ann Hiegel – Hiegel Conference Room
Andrew Remick – Remick Family Preservation Workshop
Hal & Melissa Munger – Munger Family Student Organizations Office
Jim and Colleen Ryan – Jim R. Ryan Rare Book Room
William R. Ponko

And many other donations from alumni and friends.

CREDITS

4-5 © Peter Aaron / OTTO
6-7 © Peter Aaron / OTTO
8-9 © Peter Aaron / OTTO
10-11 © Peter Aaron / OTTO
12-13 © Peter Aaron / OTTO
14 © Alexander Stoddart
16 © Andreas von Einsiedel
19 © Peter Aaron / OTTO
20 © Andreas von Einsiedel
22 © University of Notre Dame
25 © Peter Aaron / OTTO
28 © Image courtesy of Wikimedia Commons / Ssantera (16 September 2012)
29 (top left) Collection Trust / © Her Majesty Queen Elizabeth II 2020
29 (bottom left) © Andreas von Einsiedel
29 (bottom right) © Jonathan Wallen
31 (top) © Matt Cashore / University of Notre Dame
31 (centre) © Image courtesy of Wikimedia Commons / Michael Fernandes (01 May 2012)
31 (bottom) © Image courtesy of Wikimedia Commons / Adawson8 (10 April 2016)
35 (top) © Image courtesy of Wikimedia Commons / SimonWaldherr (18 May 2019)
35 (bottom) © Image courtesy of Wikimedia Commons / Ansgar Koreng (21 May 2015)
40 © Andreas von Einsiedel
57 © Peter Aaron / OTTO
59 (top) © Matt Cashore/University of Notre Dame
59 (bottom) © Peter Aaron / OTTO
60-61 © Peter Aaron / OTTO
62 © Andreas von Einsiedel
63 © Matt Cashore/University of Notre Dame
64 © Peter Aaron / OTTO
66-67 © Peter Aaron / OTTO
68 © Peter Aaron / OTTO
69 © Andreas von Einsiedel
70 © Barbara Johnston / University of Notre Dame
71 © Peter Aaron / OTTO

72 (top) © Matt Cashore/University of Notre Dame
72 (bottom) © Peter Aaron / OTTO
73 © Peter Aaron / OTTO
75 © Barbara Johnston / University of Notre Dame
77 © Peter Aaron / OTTO
78-79 © Barbara Johnston/University of Notre Dame
80 (top and bottom) © Peter Aaron / OTTO
83 © Matt Cashore/University of Notre Dame
84-85 © Matt Cashore/University of Notre Dame
87 © Peter Aaron / OTTO
89 © Matt Cashore/University of Notre Dame
90-91 © Peter Aaron / OTTO
93 Giraudon, Paris, from The Architecture of the Ecole des Beaux-Arts, ed. Arthur Drexler, with essays by Richard Chafee, Arthur Drexler, Neil Levine, and David Van Zanten, p.60
95 (top) Image courtesy of Wikimedia Commons / Jmgobet (24 September 2011)
95 (bottom) S.A.D.G. Recueil publié à l'occasion de la millième adhésion à la Société des architectes diplomés par le Gouvernement, Paris, 1911, from The Architecture of the Ecole des Beaux-Arts, ed. Arthur Drexler, with essays by Richard Chafee, Arthur Drexler, Neil Levine, and David Van Zanten, p.91
96 "Un Pailais de la Presidence dans la Capitale d'une Grande Republique." Placed Second, Grand Prix de Rome, Ecole des Beaux Arts, Paris, 1912-13, M. Gaston Castel, Pupil of M. Bernier, from The Study of Architecture of Architectural Design, by John F. Harbeson, p.120
97 Transactions of the R.I.B.A., vol. XXXIV, 1883-84, from The Architecture of the Ecole des Beaux-Arts, ed. Arthur Drexler, with essays by Richard Chafee, Arthur Drexler, Neil Levine, and David Van Zanten, p.79
98-99 © Peter Aaron / OTTO
101 © Sarah J Duncan Photography
103 © Andreas von Einsiedel
105 © Sarah J Duncan Photography

108 © June Buck Photography
112 © Andreas von Einsiedel
114-115 © Andreas von Einsiedel
116 (top) © Eton College
116 (bottom left and right) © Andreas von Einsiedel
117 © Andreas von Einsiedel
119 (top and bottom) © Andreas von Einsiedel
120 © Andreas von Einsiedel
122-123 © Andreas von Einsiedel
124 © Andreas von Einsiedel
125 © Andreas von Einsiedel
126-127 © Andreas von Einsiedel
129 © Andreas von Einsiedel
130 © June Buck Photography
133 © June Buck Photography
134 © June Buck Photography
135 © June Buck Photography
136 © June Buck Photography
137 (top and bottom) © June Buck Photography
138 © Sarah J Duncan Photography
140-41 © Sarah J Duncan Photography
142 © Sarah J Duncan Photography
143 © Sarah J Duncan Photography
144-145 © Sarah J Duncan Photography
146 © Andreas von Einsiedel
150 © Andreas von Einsiedel
151 (top and bottom) © Andreas von Einsiedel
152 (top and bottom) © Andreas von Einsiedel
153 © Andreas von Einsiedel
154-155 © Andreas von Einsiedel
156-157 © Andreas von Einsiedel
158 © Chris Heaney Photography
160 © Joanna Wachowiak
161 (top) © Chris Heaney Photography
162-163 © Joanna Wachowiak
164-165 © The Royal College of Music
167 © Andreas von Einsiedel
171 © Andreas von Einsiedel
172 © Alexander Stoddart

Previous page: Six Ionic columns support the Stoa, linking the Hall of Casts to the adjacent library wing. There is a sequence of spaces at ground floor level ranging from grand ceremonial rooms to utilitarian spaces that help students understand hierarchy and how one space can benefit from the presence of another.

Left: Preparation of the stucco original model of the Alberti statue, in Alexander Stoddart's studio at The University of the West of Scotland in Paisley, October 2018.

Page 4/5: The Hall of Casts at Walsh Family Hall is placed in the most prominent position on the site located to catch the eye on the corner of Eddy Street and Holy Cross Drive.

Page 6/7: A staircase wraps around the column of the Stoa at the east end so that the half landing is raised well above the surrounding floor to stage a speaker, much like a traditional pulpit at the end of a nave.

Page 8/9: The Library reading room, looking south towards the Leon Krier Collection across the arched tribune that rises through two levels of the library from the ground floor.

Page 10/11: View looking up at the Ionic order of the Stoa. Patterns using anthemia and palmettes decorate the ceiling between the rafters much as they would have done in a Stoa in ancient Greece.

Page 12/13: Evening view with the statue of Alberti in the foreground and the Tower and Library providing the backdrop to the court.

Page 167: The entrance to the Museum and Debating Chamber from within the new McCrum Yard at Eton College. The Sphinx Acroteria on the pediment and the Doric order from the Temple of Isis at Pompeii give a foretaste of the collection within. The Museum houses the Myers Collection of remarkable Egyptian antiquities left to the School. It serves as a place of education for the pupils and is open to visitors from outside the School. The classics master in charge refuses to provide labels identifying the exhibits on the grounds that stifles pupils' curiosity as they simply read them rather than studying the objects and speculating about them.

COLOPHON

First published in the United Kingdom
in 2021 by Triglyph Books.

Triglyph Books
154 Tachbrook Street,
London SW1V 2NE

www.TriglyphBooks.com

Designed by Steve Turner Design

British Library Cataloguing-in-Publication Data.

A catalogue record for this book is available
from the British Library.

ISBN : 978-1-9163554-2-2

Printed and bound sustainably in Italy.

THE
ACADEMY

Celebrating the work of John Simpson at the
Walsh Family Hall, University of Notre Dame, Indiana

TRIGLYPH
BOOKS